Launching a Great Year

by
Sharon Rybak

illustrated by Gary Mohrmann

Copyright © Good Apple, Inc., 1989

ISBN No. 0-86653-507-1

Printing No. 98765432

Good Apple, Inc.
Box 299
Carthage, IL 62321-0299

Dedication

To my parents, Bob and Audrey Craig. To Mom for your patience and support and to Dad for your inspiration and humor. I love you.

GA1093

Table of Contents

GA1093

GA1093

Introduction

A school year that gets off to a great start happens when teachers make very careful preparations for the beginning of the school year. The need for organization, planning and attention to the little details are all part of the opening of your classroom. This is especially true in early childhood programs where many busy young children will be actively involved with the environment. This book is designed for all early childhood teachers who are beginning a classroom for the first time or the veteran teacher who is looking for some new and fresh ideas.

As teachers begin to physically and mentally prepare for the upcoming year, they need to think of everything from finger paints, glue, crying children, parent orientations to bus schedules. It can be overwhelming! This book shares many ideas for classroom management, themes and lots of rebus pictures for your little non-readers. Many ideas are also given for organization of materials, schedules, goal setting and a First-Day Survival Kit. Novice and veteran teachers both will enjoy these valuable classroom ideas.

As you read through the book, look for little boxes called Through the Eyes of a Child. These sections give you a variety of information about child development, funny things children say, or a view of your classroom through the eyes of the children you teach. Some will give you a pause to think about a particular approach. This section helps to keep the focus on the purpose for all our work—the children we teach.

Throughout the book you will also find a section called Work Smarter, Not Harder. These ideas are developed with your busy schedule and organizational needs in mind.

I am sure you will find *Launching a Great Year* an invaluable addition to your classroom library year after year.

Ready. . .
Get Set . . .

The Beginning Theme

Two ideas for beginning themes are included in this book for your use. The first is Bubbles, Bubbles and More Bubbles and the second is Big Shoe, Little Shoe, Velcro Shoe, Tie. These themes are a break from the traditional fall or gingerbread man theme. One reason is that both of these topics lend themselves nicely to a great deal of extended learning that can include the parents and children. The bubble theme is primarily visual with an emphasis on the visual skills such as identifying colors and shapes. The shoe theme is more kinesthetic or "hands-on" with an emphasis on putting on shoes with a variety of clasps then moving up to lacing and tying.

Each theme has a Theme Song which is introduced at home and, once in school, shared as a class. This is a great way for the children to sing a new song and share it together.

Each theme also has a bulletin board and a few extended bulletin board ideas. This should culminate after the first full week of school with some sort of *special* activity.

Themes are fun but the emphasis is fun with an educational purpose. A great start is assured with involved parents and enthusiastic children.

Through the Eyes of a Child

Have you ever had to change planes quickly in a big city airport? As you exit from your first plane, your eyes scan the surroundings, and you may feel some apprehension as you attempt to find your next gate. People all seem to be rushing along and if you are alone, you may feel a bit lost or even confused. Suddenly you've stepped into a city with new signs, rules and locations. That feeling may be a small portion of the feeling young children feel as they enter a new school—everyone rushing along with a purpose, new surroundings and lots of strange signs. But adults have an advantage; they can read. As adults we have the ability to *figure out* our world through past experiences and our learned abilities. Children also need road signs that help them through the day. They need lots of patience and understanding as they attempt to proceed through the world we call school.

GA1093

Bubbles, Bubbles and More Bubbles

Dear Parents,

Our theme for the opening of school is Bubbles, Bubbles and More Bubbles. We are *bursting* into the school year with exciting ideas and new concepts for your child.

Bubbles are lots of fun but also make for great teaching opportunities. Rainbow colors and our first shape, the circle, will be just a few of the lessons. We will also discuss largest to smallest and graduated sizes. Learning in our classroom is always fun with a purpose. Your child will have the experiences that are necessary to make the lessons memorable.

Please spend some time with your child teaching this new song sung to "I'm a Little Teapot." We will sing the song on the first day of school. Your child will feel great when something familiar and shared at home is carried over to school.

Theme Song: "Bubble Magic" sung to "I'm a Little Teapot"

Here's a little bubble
Big and round
Floating high
Without a sound.

This little bubble
Won't last long so . . .
Blow some more before
It's all gone.

The letter enclosed is for your child. Please explore the activity with your child and then share other household items that might create bubbles.

More bubble magic is on the way. All of us are looking forward to working with your child and sharing the joy and excitement for learning.

Sincerely,

GA1093

Sample Letter to Child

Dear Student,

What can you make happen with dish soap, water and a bright colored rubber band? Ask Mom or Dad for help. When you come to school, we will talk about what you did with your rubber band. I will see you very soon.

Your teacher,

(Place
Rubber Band
Here.)

4

GA1093

Bubbles to Begin the Year
(A Visual Approach)
Bursting into School

Bulletin Board

The children will cut out their own circle and can glue on a rectangle of aluminum foil for the reflection.

Ideas to Put on Your Bubbles:

- a bubble wish dictated by the child
- the child's name
- paint with watercolors
- a photo of the child
- large bubbles for morning class and smaller for afternoon or two different colors

Notes and quotes and all communication can be inside the bubbles.

GA1093

Little Bubble Makers

Consider sending each child home with a container of bubbles after your orientation. Encourage children to try different things to make bubbles. Ask them to bring in their most unusual bubble-making tool the first day of school.

Don't forget to sing the bubble theme song.

"Bubble Magic" sung to "I'm a Little Teapot"

Here's a little bubble
Big and round
Floating high
Without a sound.

This little bubble
Won't last long so . . .
Blow some more before
It's all gone.

Double Bubble Name Tags

HI!
MY NAME IS

GA1093

Snack for Orientation

Homemade bread with lots of bubbles in the bread.

The bread can be made in class, or the teacher can use the prepared bread dough in the dairy department of the grocery store. The following is a simple bread recipe:

2½ cups (605 ml) warm water
2 packages dry yeast
4 tablespoons (60 ml) soft shortening

4 teaspoons (20 ml) salt
4 tablespoons (60 ml) sugar
6 cups (1440 ml) sifted flour

Dissolve yeast in warm water. Add salt, sugar and shortening. Add half the flour. Let half the children mix this mixture with a large spoon. Add the rest of the flour and let the remaining children mix by hand. Floured hands work best. Let rise 30 minutes. Pat down and put in a greased loaf pan. Pat with floured hands. Let rise. Bake at 375° F (191° C) for 40 minutes.

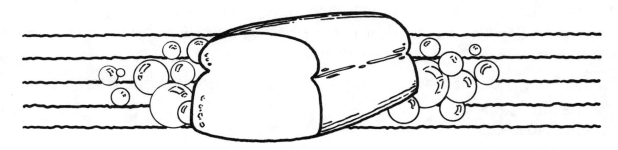

After School Starts

- Bubble gum blowing (sugarfree)
- Bubble making using straws, cups, hoola hoops, pop can plastic tops and lots, lots more.
- Kick off ideas for units on colors, shapes (can you make a triangle bubble?), prisms and rainbows.

GA1093

Big Shoe, Little Shoe, Velcro Shoe, Tie

Dear Parents,

Our theme for the opening of school is Big Shoe, Little Shoe, Velcro Shoe, Tie. We are "lacing" up some exciting ideas and new concepts for your child.

Working with shoes is lots of fun but also makes for great teaching opportunities. Our first activity will allow us to graph the different types of shoes worn in our classroom and compare the styles and numbers in each group. We will also work on lacing skills and compare various shoe sizes, using words like *big*, *bigger* and *biggest*. Learning in our classroom is always fun with a purpose. Your child will have the experiences that are necessary to make the lessons memorable.

Please spend some time with your child teaching this new song sung to "Twinkle, Twinkle, Little Star." We will sing the song on the first day of school. Your child will feel great when something familiar and shared at home is carried over to school.

Theme Song: "Some Shoes" sung to "Twinkle, Twinkle, Little Star"

Some shoes buckle
Some shoes clip
Some shoes zip
And zap they rip.

Some shoes Velcro
Some shoes tie
Some shoes hurt
And some won't tie.

Some shoes seem
Like all the rest
But my new shoes
Are sure the best.

The letter enclosed is for your child. Please explore the activity with your child and then share other things around the house that your child might lace or tie.

More shoe fun is on the way. All of us are looking forward to working with your child and sharing the joy and excitement of learning.

Sincerely,

GA1093

Sample Letter to Child

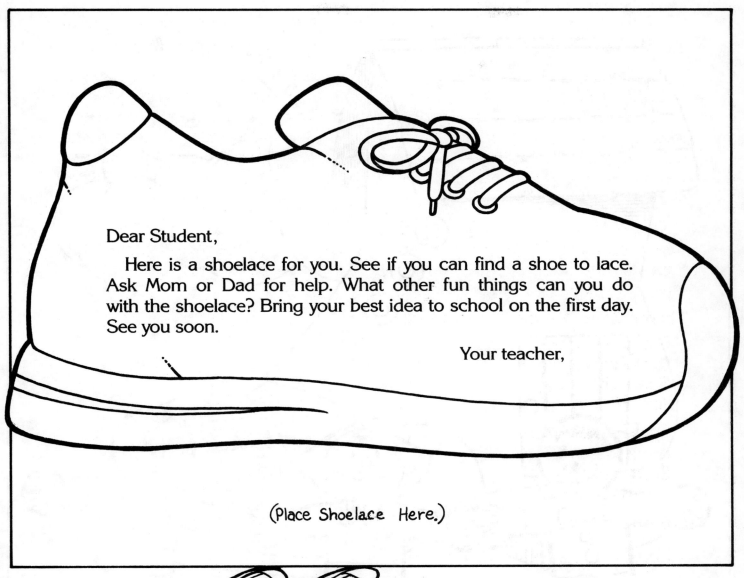

Dear Student,

   Here is a shoelace for you. See if you can find a shoe to lace. Ask Mom or Dad for help. What other fun things can you do with the shoelace? Bring your best idea to school on the first day. See you soon.

                              Your teacher,

(Place Shoelace Here.)

GA1093

Big Shoe, Little Shoe, Velcro Shoe, Tie

(A Kinesthetic Approach)

The teacher will prepare simple paper dolls and leave them together or cut them apart. Each child will color and decorate his/her person and place it around the shoe.

10

GA1093

Theme song: "Some Shoes" sung to "Twinkle, Twinkle, Little Star"

Some shoes buckle
Some shoes clip
Some shoes zip
And zap they rip.

Some shoes Velcro
Some shoes tie
Some shoes hurt
And some won't tie.

Some shoes seem
Like all the rest
But my new shoes
Are sure the best.

Other Shoe Activities

- Discuss other things that come in pairs.
- Learn the parts of the shoe such as heel and sole.
- Make prints using the interesting patterns on the bottoms of old tennis shoes.
- Keep various types of shoes in a basket for trying on and imaginary play.
- Discuss left and right shoes.
- A real shoe nailed to a small wooden board makes the best tool for teaching how to tie.
- Visit a shoe store.
- Invite in a shoemaker or shoe repairman to school.

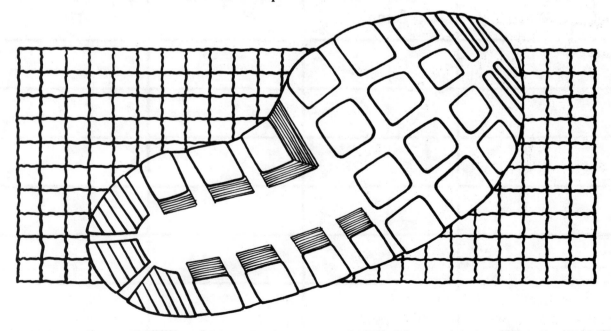

GA1093

Shoe Name Tags

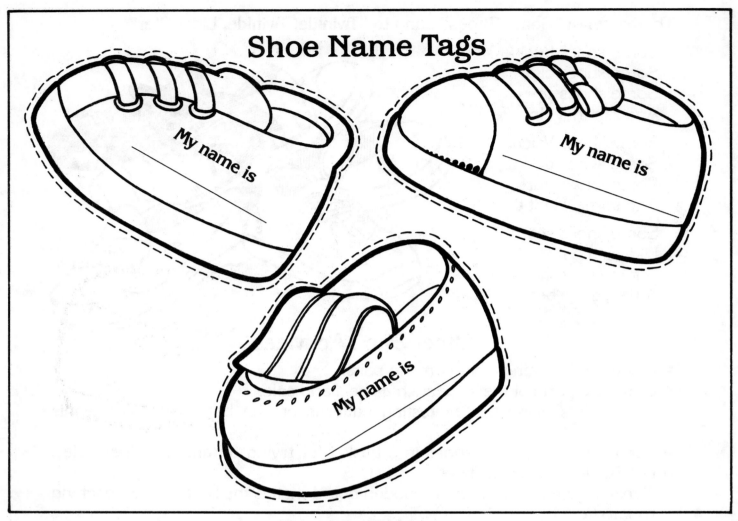

My name is _____

My name is _____

My name is _____

Shoe Graph

Velcro	Buckle	Slip-on	Tie

GA1093

Shoes for Shoe Graph

Have each child choose the shoe type that he/she is wearing. Color and cut out the shoe type and add it to the shoe graph. Count the number of shoes in each column and then compare the columns to each other. Which has more, less, how many more and how many all together?

GA1093

Bulletin Board Ideas That Include Children's Work

Bulletin boards are places in the classroom that display children's work. These bulletin board ideas are designed to have complete class participation, using the most simplistic designs. Young children may not be ready for a complicated art project, but most are ready to color and others are ready for cutting, tracing and pasting. It is up to the teacher to upgrade or downgrade the activity based on the ability of the students in the class.

Our School of Children

Have each of the children trace a simple fish and include it in the fishbowl.

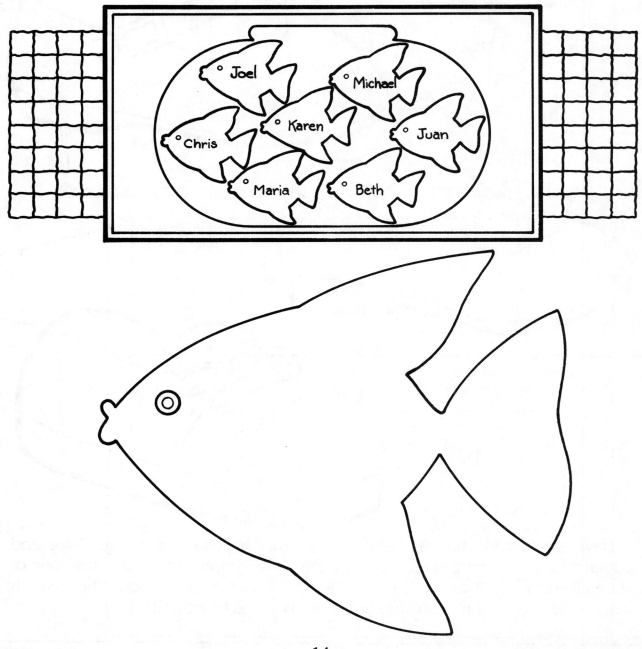

Colorful Class

After each child has made a crayon, the crayons are placed in the box by the teacher. This can further be developed into printing the color word on the crayon.

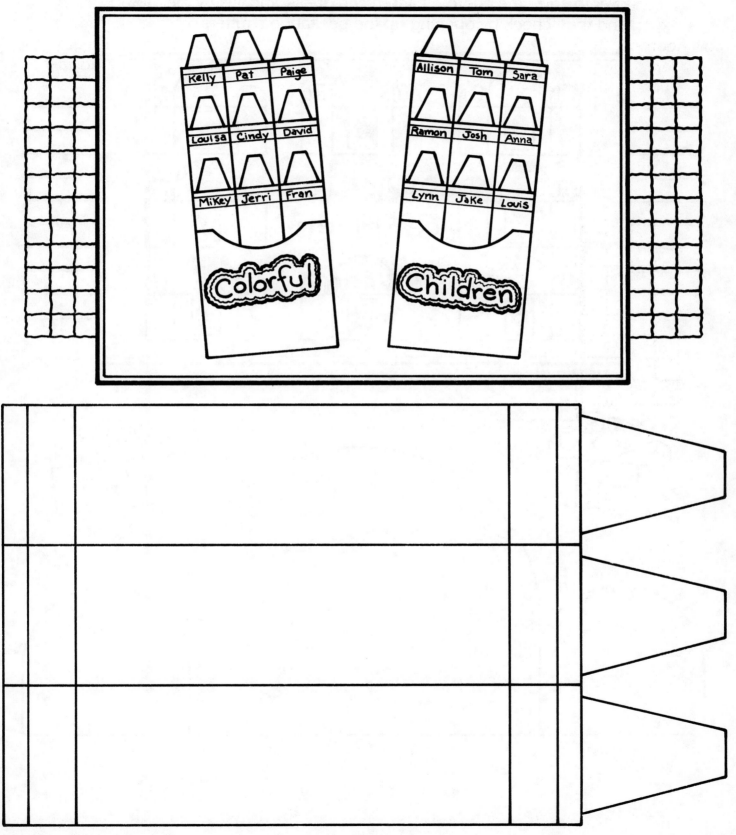

                                                   GA1093

Peekaboo Children

The children will color in the heads and hands to create themselves. The piece of paper will hold a photograph of the child taken on the first day of school. The sides of the paper will fold over to cover the photo. Children can guess who it is by the drawing and then check by opening up the peekaboo shutters.

GA1093

Ice-Cream Cone

Use an illustration of a giant animal next to a giant ice-cream cone. Each child will cut out one of the scoops and the teacher will complete the giant ice-cream cone.

17

GA1093

Look at Me!

During the orientation, the teacher takes photos of the children with the parent or guardian. Mount the pictures on paper apples which then are put on the Happy Apple Tree.

Having the picture of a familiar face is a comfort for the child, and it helps the teacher associate the parents with the children.

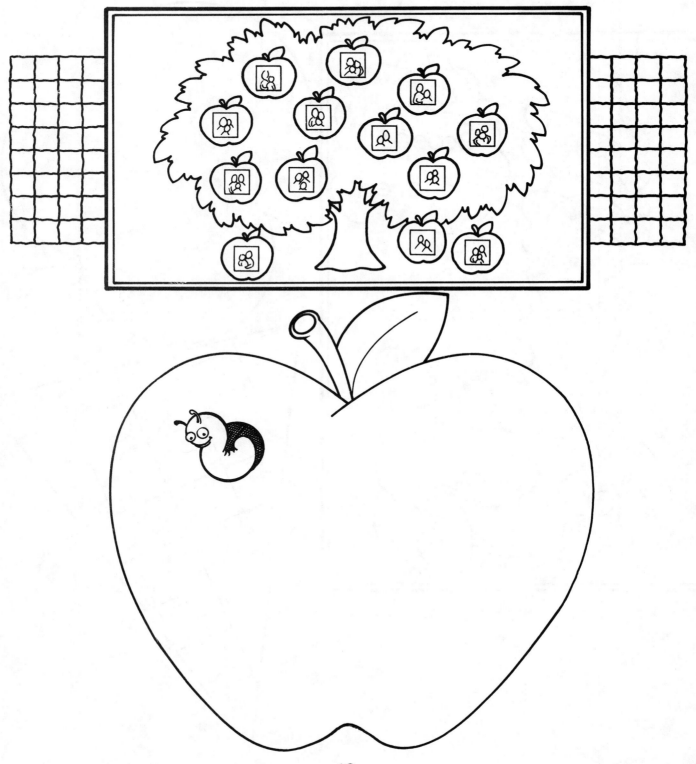

GA1093

Rainbows

Place an illustration of a giant rainbow across the middle of the bulletin board. The morning class can create the raindrops, and the afternoon class can create bows that float around the bottom creating RAIN-BOWS.

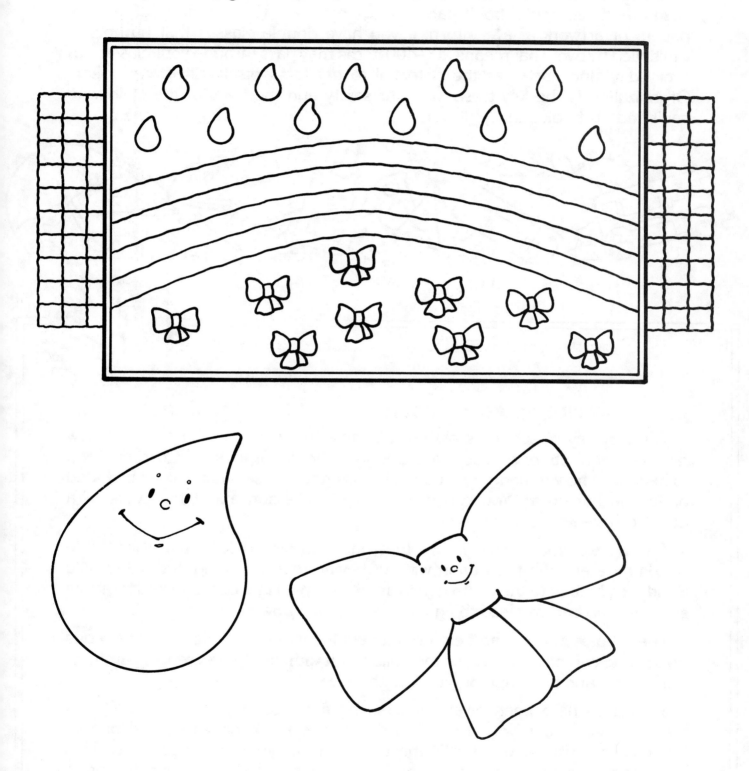

GA1093

"Hey, That's My Locker"
Organization of a Child's Personal Materials

When 25 children enter your classroom, they bring with them 25 coats, scarfs, mittens, boots, book bags and gym shoes. They produce 25 sets of papers or artwork at every turn. If you have double classes that number is multiplied by two. That means 200-400 items may pass through your classroom every day, and each has the potential to get lost, misidentified, or broken. Organization is the key to saving your sanity and the tears of the child who can't find his book bag.

Work Smarter, Not Harder—Ideas for Coats

The first day of school is always a bit tougher if it rains. That means new rain gear and lots of practice with using our hooks or lockers. Children need to be taught how to hang up a coat. Discuss how to use a chain if it's provided or to use the collar. You can even lead off a lesson about the parts of a coat from sleeves to lining to hem.

If you have hooks, make sure that one is provided for each child. Little hands have enough frustration without having to share a big and little hook. Send the children to the coatroom in small groups. Tight quarters and territory-sensitive children can lead to fights. "He knocked down my coat."

The rebus symbols can help nonreaders identify their space. Put the rebus on the back of the name tag so the child has it with him for reference. Laminate the symbol and then tape or glue it to the area.

If children have been given lockers, the first lesson will be how to open the door. For many young children this may take some time. Find one or two children who have this skill mastered, and they can be your locksmiths. The second lesson is that all items must be inside before closing the door. This will eliminate the dreaded "locker jam."

GA1093

List of Rebus Symbols (40)

flower	car	heart	pig
sun	lion	bus	sheep
moon	monkey	shoe	cow
tree	horse	balloon	bell
bee	frog	fish	butterfly
bird	apple	scissors	snail
dog	cupcake	penguin	rabbit
cat	crayon	squirrel	zebra
star	pencil	rainbow	strawberry
house	snowman	book	cherry

GA1093

22

GA1093

Work Smarter, Not Harder

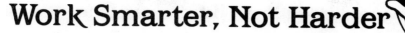

The Extras—Scarfs, Hats, Mittens

Just like the three little kittens, these are the lost items that almost always get misplaced. The reason is that they don't have a place. Some children like to put these items in their book bags; but if you are carrying a stuffed animal for show and tell, it can get a bit tough to fit everything inside. One way to keep things together is to shove the items down the coat sleeves. This is good for two reasons. One, the child cannot get his coat on without being confronted with the other items that need to also be worn home; second, in most cases the items won't fall out of the coat. It also leaves the book bag empty for the art projects and papers going home.

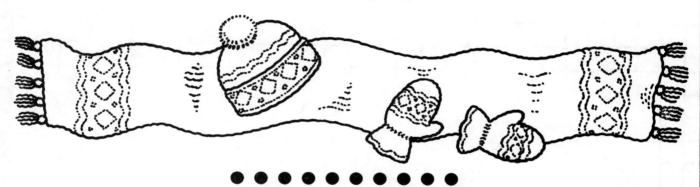

● ● ● ● ● ● ● ● ● ●

Book Bags

Since children started to school, there has always been some form of book carrying. Today the industry is enormous, and children can carry everything from doll to dinosaur book bags. The problem is that many people who design the bags don't field-test with small children. A teacher standing alone with twenty-five children who can't zip, snap, buckle or mount the book bags on their backs can be overwhelming. If school is the place to learn independence, then children need to have the appropriate materials to get them off to a nonfrustrating start. Encourage parents to buy bags that are not too small or difficult for their child to maneuver.

GA1093

Boots

Boots can be one of the most difficult things for young children when it comes to getting ready for a snowy day. Here are a few tips that might ease the way.

Boots that go over shoes need plastic bags over the shoe to ease the shoe into the boot. The plastic bags from the produce section of the grocery store work the best.

Bright red nail polish on the insole of the boots helps with left and right. The "lips" have to "kiss" in order for the boots to be ready to be worn.

Snap-on clothespins in a pail by the coat area remind the children that they need to snap their boots together after taking them off. This helps eliminate the wrong size-same style dilemma.

GA1093

Papers—Bulletins—Art Projects

Children need to have a place for their paper belongings. This can be a mailbox made from a cardboard shoe holder to a folder. Here are some ideas for classroom-generated materials.

Make sure the location of the mailbox or cubby has the same rebus symbol for easy identification.

Make sure that the child can easily reach the location and that it is not in a heavily congested area. Remember that twenty-five children will move through this area at least once a day and maybe more.

Hang art pictures on a clothes rack and let the children take their pictures from the rack as they go to leave the classroom.

Hand back papers and bulletins as the children leave the classroom. This eliminates having to stuff mailboxes.

Completed and checked papers can be immediately put in the mailboxes by the children. Only collect papers that need more time to examine.

Quick-check correcting can be done by moving from table to table around the room. Make sure you sit down and don't bend over tables all day. It will tire you quickly and take a toll on your back.

Three-dimensional art projects or large projects can be clipped on to a sturdy clothesline to finish drying. This will also get them out of the way of busy hands and feet.

GA1093

"Too Much Stuff"
Organization of the Teacher's Personal Material

Which do you need more. . .

- one more Halloween or

- a place to put all your Halloween ideas?

Teachers have a host of activities from which to choose in the preparation of their lessons. Commerical materials, books and file boxes with prepared materials are all available with useful and creative ideas. The problem is that the ideas need to be organized so they can be resourced when needed.

The best advice for any organization system is to keep up with whatever system you choose. Work on developing, cleaning and updating your file system. Here are a few organizational systems that might work for your classroom.

File by Subject

Some teachers keep a file for each letter of the alphabet and each number taught. You can also file your materials by subject and special units. Each of these files can be housed in separate file folders. These would then be put in filing cabinets. The only problem with this system is that much of the material for early childhood is three-dimensional and gets bulky in folders.

File by Month or Season

Another system is to keep boxes with lids for each month. This is beneficial because the teacher can keep files and miscellaneous materials together. The bunny pin, plastic Easter eggs, honeycombed flowers and the oversized art projects can all be stored within the box.

If you take your materials home or store them in a remote place when completed, make sure you keep out two months worth of files at a time. You will continue to find things in November that belong in the October files.

GA1093

Oversized Posters and Cutouts

As the years go by, we collect more and more materials that become difficult storage problems. One method of storage is to use the large storage boxes that fit under beds. Another is to use large sheets of tagboard or cardboard bound with strapping tape to keep the materials flat. Very flat boxes such as these can be hung on the back of cupboard doors or fit between cabinets.

Keep on the Lookout

When you see an idea in one of your books or magazines, go to the copy machine and make a copy and file the idea even if you own the book. If the idea is too long to copy, just copy the first page and then file the idea. This way when you are ready to teach you will have the materials at your fingertips and won't need to look through your books for ideas.

As you prepare for the coming school year, plan the units and themes that you will be teaching and keep a list near your desk and a file folder for each idea in your drawer. As you read magazines and overview material, you will see ideas, posters and hands-on materials that will support these units. By the time the unit is ready to be taught, the materials will be available.

GA1093

Teacher's Desk

Besides all the regular materials you keep in your desk area, consider these additions:

- A bulletin board with schedules, weekly bulletins, family pictures, notes to send home and things to remember.

- A drawer for your students to access. Helper hands can help themselves to tape, pointed scissors when needed, chalk, rubber bands, paper clips, markers, safety pins, stapler, hole punch, etc. This will save you steps and allow children the freedom to use alternative materials when needed.

- A few things you may have forgotten:

rubber cement	stripping tape
ribbon	matches
stamp pad	thank-you notes
good set of markers	needle and thread
vase for flowers	extra panty hose
loose change	X-acto knife
hot glue gun	

GA1093

Organization of Classroom Supplies

- There is no more black paper.
- The glue is stuck and will not come out of the container.
- The paint has dried up at the easel.
- The finger paint pictures are all stuck together.
- The clay is as hard as rocks.
- The brushes have been left and are dried and misshapen.
- Pencils and crayons are broken and missing.

These kinds of problems are a real part of the organization in an early childhood classroom. Teachers sometimes feel they spend too much time just working on the care and cleaning of classroom supplies. With proper organization and some cooperation from children, the management of these materials can become easier.

Pencils

Two cups by the pencil sharpener with dull pencils in one cup and sharp pencils in the other can help your lost, dull or broken pencil problem. The child who is given the job of pencil sharpening is to sharpen the pencils in the dull cup every morning and put them in the sharp cup. Anyone needing a sharpened pencil may take one from the sharp cup but must first put a pencil in the dull cup. This sytem keeps track of lost pencils and also doesn't use class time for pencil sharpening.

GA1093

Crayons

Boxes, no boxes, fat crayons, skinny crayons, whole crayons, broken crayons, "I don't have a green crayon."

Crayon organization is a must! It seems like a small problem until you have missing colors and aggravation over lost or missing crayons or crayon boxes.

Can System

Some teachers like to put the crayons in juice cans and sort the crayons by color. Large juice cans hold about eight fat crayons. Each child can have his/her own can or each table can have a basket with eight containers and a color in each container. The advantage to this system is it helps with the organization skills. The children must sort their crayons into the appropriate can after every use. The disadvantage is that the cans dump and mix together. As the crayons become broken, it also becomes difficult to reach in the can for the crayons.

Box System

Many teachers like to keep the crayons in their original box. This works well, but the boxes will be broken down before the crayons will be gone. If you want the boxes to hold their shape, reinforce them with stripping tape.

Basket System

Some teachers put all the crayons in a basket and let the children take a crayon as needed. This is actually good for visual discrimination, easy and less structured. The disadvantage is that it does not nurture individual responsibility for belongings.

Decide if you are trying to convey something with your organization or are you trying to get the materials in the children's hands. If children need to share, make sure they have easy access and do not need to share with more than three other children.

GA1093

Fat Versus Skinny Crayons—the Debate Continues

The truth is fat crayons were created to help teachers who complained of broken crayons. There is no significant evidence that says fat crayons are easier or better for little hands. As a matter of fact, they may be more difficult to manage than their smaller counterpart. If you plan to give children small detailed work and large crayons, you are courting disaster and lots of aggravation from Little Mary Sunshine who loves to color. On the other hand, the child who moves his whole arm while coloring may find them useful in covering a broader area.

A good solution is to allow for choice. Provide both types and let the children decide which works best for that particular activity.

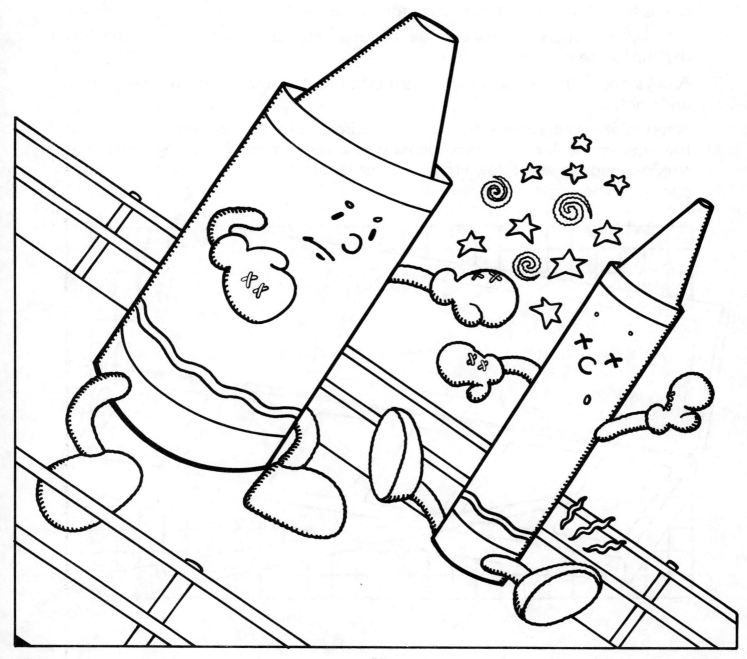

GA1093

Paints

Dry Tempera: When you prepare dry tempera, add some liquid starch to thicken the paint and smooth the flow. Also add a squirt of liquid detergent to help the cleanup process.

Don't try to make too much paint mixture ahead of its needed use because it does spoil and will let off an unpleasant odor.

Collect various containers to help in the preparation process. Half-gallon milk or juice containers can be used for mixing and storage refills for the week.

Premixed Tempera: This type of paint can be convenient, but it can also cause some problems. Large containers will often settle and have paint the consistency of mud resting at the bottom. It can be difficult to remove and needs to be thinned and mixed in order to be used.

Smaller containers get used faster but may also get very thick and equally difficult to use.

Always check the lids and wipe them clean to make sure they are on square and tight.

Watercolors: Watercolors are fun for children, but they frequently muddy the tray and mix colors. An easy cleanup is a quick run of the tray under the sink running the water down from lightest to darkest.

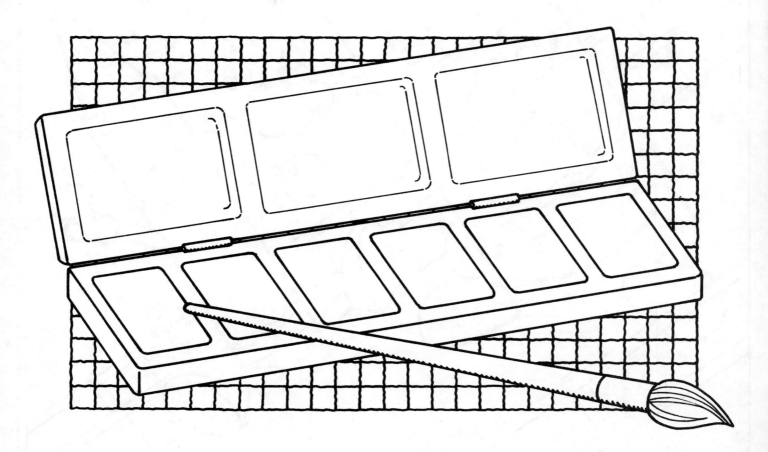

GA1093

Easel Paint Setup

Preparing the Area: An old shower curtain taped to the floor is a good cover when setting up your easel center. Any type of plastic that is heavy will work as well. Cover the trays where the paints rest with aluminum foil. It easily molds to the trays and makes for quick and easy cleanup when needed. The easel areas themselves can be covered with small kitchen garbage bags.

The most efficient containers for paint are the commercially purchased cups with inverted cones and lids. These allow the children to wipe their brushes on the inverted cone as they pull them from the cup. This lightens the paint load on the brush. The lids and containers are sturdy and resistant to spills when dropped.

When you plan your containers for the easel center, assume that at some time or another that one or more of those containers will be dumped or dropped. If it is an open container, fill it only as high as you want to clean— the more paint, the more cleaning. Young children can help but should not be expected to clean a full blown fallout. It is better to refill the containers every day than have a major cleanup of student and room.

Each container with the colors must have its own paintbrush. Sharing a brush between containers makes for gray paints.

GA1093

Finger Paints

Commercially made finger paints hold up very well and last a long time. Other mediums are pudding and shaving cream for fun pictures. Let the children finger-paint on the table and create a scene. Blot the picture that is created with a piece of paper. Encourage swirls with tiny fingers, and when the print is dry, let the children color the swirls with colored chalk. This creates a beautiful ribbon effect. Children should be encouraged to clean up their own mess using good sponges and paper towels.

Cleanup

Soaking the brushes and containers is the easiest cleanup. A weekend in soapy water will soften dry paint and make the job a great deal easier. Keep lots of small pails on hand and use gloves when it comes time for paint container cleanup.

Smocks

Dad's old shirts have been an early childhood standby for a generation of Picassos. A new twist can be added. On the front of the shirt use a hot glue gun and attach Velcro strips for easy dressing. Little paint-soaked fingers will only need to give a pull to remove the shirt.

GA1093

That Sticky Stuff—Glue—the Dilemma

Today's choices for classroom adhesives are extensive. Teachers can choose from sticks, pastes or white glues. In different situations each may be appropriate.

Nothing is so sad as a child whose beloved project falls apart before he/she gets it home. Make sure the adhesives you use in your classroom become a teaching tool, not a teaching headache.

Glue

White Glue: White glue holds well and allows children the opportunity to hopefully stay clean while they are working. The problem is many young children overdose their pictures with too much glue. Here is a teaching technique that will help your children control the flow.

Use dot-to-dot pictures in a learning center. This is best taught in small groups. Tell children they must control the flow of the glue and put a dot on each dot of the picture. Teach how to open, squeeze with control, clean and close the containers. This little lesson will save the teacher time and aggravation. When you expect children to glue pictures, just give them a number. Four dots and they will understand your expectations.

The newest of inventions for dispensing a drop of glue is Tape & Glue. Tape & Glue was invented by a kindergarten teacher. It attaches to the top of any standard glue container and allows for only one drop of glue to be dispensed at a time.*

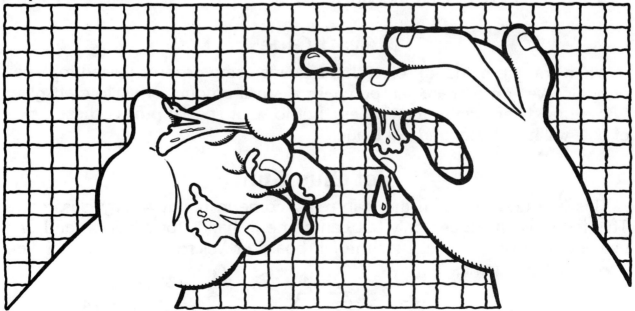

*Tape & Glue, Leech Products, Inc., P.O. Box 2147, Hutchinson, KS 67504-2147 or phone 1-800-992-9018.

GA1093

Glue Sticks

The newest of the adhesives for children can be best utilized when children are working independently. Glue sticks hold light objects and paper and are carefree for the teacher whose children are working alone.

Paste

Paste has a few applicator dilemmas that need to be addressed.

Fingers: Children can use their fingers to apply the paste from most containers. Some teachers put small amounts on paper or plastic lids for the children's daily use. This works well but for some children it becomes a whole-arm type of activity. Finger spreading may also frustrate children with poor motor control because it gives them sticky hands.

Tongue Depressors: Tongue depressors make great paste or glue spreaders. Tongue depressors will stick together if you use white glue. Some teachers use coffee stirrers for this purpose also.

Brushes: Some paste containers have brushes. These work well when new but as they get older they may be more difficult. Many of these brushes also don't reach the bottom of the container.

Paste dries in the containers easily and needs consistent monitoring to check for tight lids. Excess paste like excess glue can cause for heavy, wet pictures. When using paste, buy small containers and fill them frequently. The more they are filled the less likely they are to dry up.

Craft Glue

When you are doing a project that requires using peanuts pasted to paper or jiggle eyes on a character, purchase a small amount of white craft glue. Some brands are better than others, but for that special project these types of glue will hold better and last longer.

Hot Glue Gun

This is a new invention that can really come in handy in any classroom. This is for teacher's use only but can come in handy for a million and one uses—gluing on felt backs for the felt board or Velcro strips, fixing broken toys or making games.

Other Holders

Children need experiences and practice using other office materials. Here are a few with the rules for usage.

Paper Clips: Paper clips and playing cards make a challenging exercise for little hands. Rule: Don't bend the clip out of shape. Slide it on.

Hole Punch and Brass Paper Brads: Let children punch holes and use brass fasteners to hold the papers together. They can assemble their own books. Xerox the pages with the hole mark indicated. Let them punch and then brad their books together. Rule: Catch the holes you make in a paper plate.

Rubber Bands: Playing cards and rubber bands make an excellent experience for children who need control over their eye-hand coordination. Rule: Bands stay on the table and near the cards, not in the air.

Stickpins: Large stickpins and a corkboard make game playing fun. Make sure you have exactly enough pins for the process to play the game. Matching is good for this area. Rule: The end of the pin goes only in the board, nowhere else!

Stapler: With practice children can learn to use the stapler and staple papers and use with art projects. Rule: All hands on top of the stapler—no fingers underneath.

The best part about all of these activities is that they are excellent for eye-hand coordination and children feel that they are sharing the tools.

GA1093

Scissors

Scissors: Proper use of scissors requires a flowing open and shut motion. For some little hands, cutting with scissors requires total concentration and mental reminders to open and close with each stroke.

Leading Up to Scissors Use: Teachers should play games that require children to open and shut their hands and fingers repeatedly. Any songs about alligators will work just fine. Follow these activities with open and shutting tools like tweezers, barbecue tongs and strawberry huskers. These are fun for all picking up beads, blocks, cereal, etc.

Types of Scissors: The new plastic safety scissors work very well because they conform to left or right-handed children. This type of scissors also holds up well and doesn't rust and stick like the older metal counterpart. If you do have metal scissors, keep them dry and with any type of scissors keep them clean for better use.

Holding and Cutting with Scissors: Many children need to be reminded which finger goes where when first learning to cut. One of the biggest mistakes is that small children flip their thumbnail down. Remind the children that their thumbnail is always on top.

Start with simple snipping which allows for one cut to completion. That should be moved to a continued line and then to curves and circles for cutting practice.

Children love to fringe paper, cut paper straws and cut pictures from magazines. Let the experiences be open-ended and then move to cutting shapes, lines and eventually snowflakes.

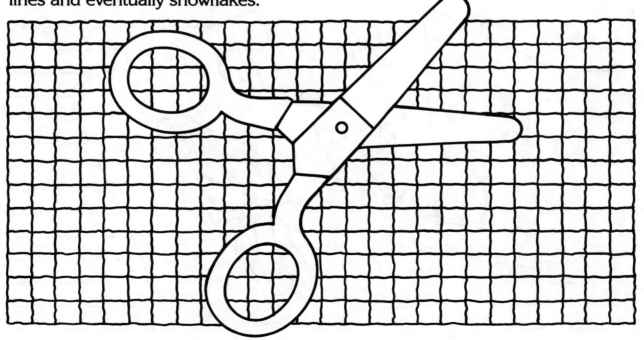

GA1093

Storage Materials

A place for everything and everything in its place—a tough job in a classroom with small children. One of the keys to good organization is good storage. Below is a short list of resources for storage that you may find helpful.

- inexpensive plastic baskets
- strawberry baskets
- bushel baskets
- laundry baskets
- Easter baskets
- coin purses for small game pieces
- plastic bags
- shoe boxes
- juice cans
- ice-cream containers from ice-cream stores
- containers from the school cafeteria
- circle rings to lock materials together
- gallon and half-gallon milk containers cut in half

The containers should be sturdy, safe and labeled with the items they contain. They should also be visible and easy for the child to carry and manipulate.

Don't Overstock: Provide just enough materials for a particular child to accomplish the task over a five-minute period. If too many objects appear in the basket, the child will sense a lack of ability to finish and quit.

GA1093

Learning Centers

Every teacher has a mental image of Mrs. Wonderful's classroom where every child is quietly working on a beautiful center made by the teacher. The room is organized and quiet and every child is on task. The environment is enriched with carpets and soft chairs, and the room is so large that the children have ample room to stretch out on the floor.

This is not reality! Reality is an environment with real children where there is often limited space and limited resources. Children make noise and teachers scramble to find a space for anything extra.

Learning centers can exist in any environment. Learning centers are appropriate with every group of children. Centers don't need to be elaborate to be effective. Learning centers are places where children can go to explore and enrich their experiences.

Centers don't need a great deal of additional material for the classroom. Traditional classroom materials can be used in a variety of ways without the necessity of making extensive materials.

Centers can be implemented without a great deal of additional planning and organization time on the part of the teacher.

Centers can be anywhere at any time. A plant on the window or a bug on the wall can turn into a center. Centers are opportunities to share, to explore and to learn.

The following section on centers will share ideas on how to create an exciting environment without elaborate planning and extraordinary effort.

The Value of Centers

Learning centers—what do they do and why do we need them?

1. Experiences that reinforce through repetition!

   Repetition of newly acquired information is essential if it is to be remembered and integrated. For future skill building, children must have a solid foundation. That foundation is built when children are taught through a variety of modes and with opportunities for repetition.

2. The value of discovery:

   When children discover the information for themselves, they have engaged in a variety of experiences that extend beyond the information gathered. Discovery provides for self-actualization and ownership over the information.

3. Evaluation and correction:

   Making mistakes and modeling behaviors is part of learning. Evaluation and correction are necessary elements to quality processing. Children must be allowed to make mistakes and fix their mistakes without fear of failure. Learning centers give opportunities to engage in joint ventures and open-ended activities that promote risk taking.

4. A kinesthetic approach:

   Centers allow children the ability to see things up close. They need to see them, touch them, move them, share them and make them their own.

5. Allowing for choice:

   When children make a choice they make a commitment. That choice gives the child ownership and will encourage and stimulate learning.

GA1093

Through the Eyes of a Child

Have you ever gone to a workshop and gotten closed out of a session you particularly wanted to attend? You may choose a different session but regret missing the desired session. You might feel angry and not pay particular attention at the session you are attending. When we are denied or directed against our wishes, we balk. Children operate in exactly the same manner. They have desires, plans and opinions. They may reject our constant direction or become complacent and lose initiative.

Too much direction and overzealous organization can be the one thing that kills learning centers for teachers and for children. Many teachers spend more time *scheduling* the centers than it takes the children to *do* the centers.

The children are herded through the centers where a limited amount of time is given before a change is required and no allowances are made for personal choice or preference.

Center Organization

Here are two alternatives for center organization that require no advanced preparation on the part of the teacher and give children a chance to make choices.

1. Your Choice
   Ask the children what they want to do. If you have conflicts, teach negotiation skills. These are perfect opportunities for lessons in compromise.

2. Pocket People
   - Make a chart for each center with the correct number of library pockets attached that match the number of children who can attend the centers.
   - Provide cards for the children with their names printed across the top. (Let the children print their names if possible.)

GA1093

The children can move from center to center and carry their cards. As each child leaves the center he/she must mark the card with a specific color that matches the center or stamp the card with a specific stamp. If a pocket isn't available then the child knows that it is a closed center until someone leaves. The teacher can record the children's attendance, if necessary, by the colors or stamps on the cards.

If a teacher needs to work with a child in a specific center, then the card is placed at that center at the beginning of the day by the teacher.

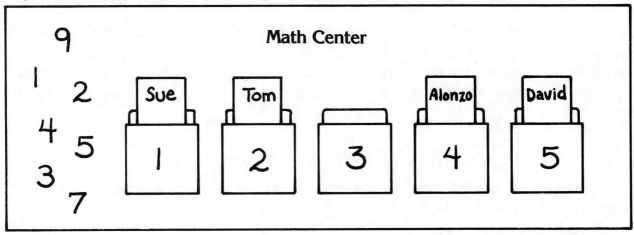

No One Will Work at the Difficult Centers?

Many times children who resist a new center, resist because they are unsure of the activity and may be afraid of failure. The teacher needs to pair the child with a "doer" or the teacher needs to join the child at the center and share the activity.

What if no one will work at a particular center? Is the center designed for success? Does it have appeal?

● ● ● ● ● ● ● ● ● ● ●

Through the Eyes of a Child

In a roomful of centers designed for educators, very few of us would choose the physics center. Physics, me? But what if that center had balls and popguns, dolls and Hot Wheels? All the objects at the center demonstrated each of the physics concepts. Each educator could manipulate the materials and learn the concept in a nonthreatening environment.

Very few children will run from the concepts—they will run from the design, format or presentation!

Learning Tools

The manipulatives needed for center exploration can be from a variety of resources and fall into a variety of categories.

- Traditional early childhood play materials such as blocks, playhouse, paints, etc.
- Small manipulatives such as puzzles, beads, inch cubes, etc.
- Prepared center materials such as games, flip cards, matching games, etc.
- Other materials such as books, computers, musical instruments, clay, etc.

All of these materials need to be experienced on the exploration level. Children need to have open-ended experiences with these materials before they are expected to learn a concept using the materials. As children become acquainted with the materials, the teacher can then introduce the curriculum skills in the centers.

Centers That Teach Work Skills

The centers themselves should teach various work and organizational skills. As the centers are developed, the design should allow the teacher to introduce these various types of skills.

- Sequential skills (example—Do steps 1-2-3)
- Two separate activities (example—Listen and Do)
- Messy and cleanup centers
- Cooperation centers (example—games that require taking turns)
- Rebus directions (example—symbols for cut and paste)

As the centers are introduced, the different types of rules and expectations will be discussed.

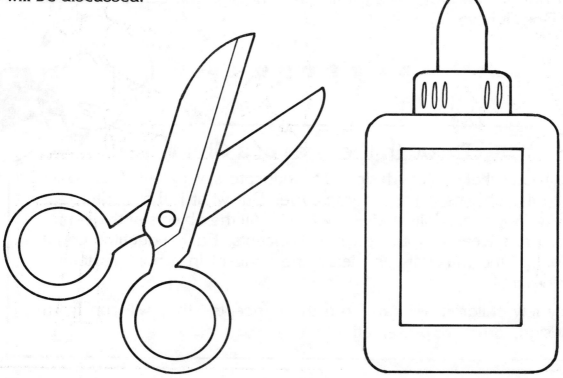

Room Environment

Centers make noise. Here is a checklist to gauge the noise level and tell what is happening in your room.

GOING well . . . . The children are working with materials and talking to each other.

The children are raising their voices and sharing answers.

still GOING well . . . . . The children are moving throughout the room talking about materials.

The children are showing excitement for the centers and the volume is raised.

GONE! The children are yelling across the room at each other.

The children are running from center to center and are not directed.

The children are using the materials in an inappropriate way.

Remember every voice belongs to a person. The more people, the more noise—productive or not! Listen to the quality of the noise and then stop and listen to the conversations. Is the noise related to the activities? If so, then your room is working productively.

GA1093

Work Smarter, Not Harder—Ideas for Listening Centers

Have you ever locked yourself in a closet and tried to tape a story for your classroom? The phone rings, the dog barks or you flub a word—forget it!

Tape your lessons as you teach them. As you read a story, put the tape recorder on your lap. If you do a rhyming lesson, tape it and let the tape be a review at the center. A cute little lesson on directional words can be placed at a gross motor activity center. The best part is that the lesson is already introduced, taught and ready to put into use.

Headphones

Do you spend a portion of your center time trying to unknot the earphone cords? Do some children zap the volume on full force and blast their center mates? Do you have children who are constantly saying, "I can't hear." Get rid of the headphones! Earphones are an unnatural phenomenon. If we could teach all children with headphones on and talk into each little ear, they might be more appropriate.

In reality, children must learn to listen and filter out distractions. A low-volume tape in the corner of the room is more appropriate and children will enjoy the freedom to move and not have the pressure of the headphones on their ears.

● ● ● ● ● ● ● ● ● ● ●

Through the Eyes of a Child

If it was the nature of children to avoid change, never challenge themselves and only look for the easy way out, not one of our children would walk, talk or be bathroom trained to mention only a few skills learned. Children's innate sense tells them to keep trying even when they fall on their knees and bloody their noses. Every child sets out to learn, explore and grow from birth. What happens to children who lose the sense of discovery and stop asking why or express fear of change? Have they been taught that there is only one correct way? Has the message been sent that they are not capable of making quality decisions? As humans grow and learn to become a master in any field, they do it through self-initiation, determination and persistent repetition of the skill. Learning centers provide the framework for mastery of concepts within the curriculum.

Rebus Symbols for Learning Centers

Symbols for:

cut	scissors
paste	glue
color	crayon
draw	pencil drawing a figure
write	pencil writing a letter
see teacher	teacher
listen	ears
tell	child with bubble from mouth like a cartoon
stop	stop sign
paint	paintbrush
put in order	little house with number 1, bigger 2, biggest 3
look	eyes
don't look	eyes with ✕
cleanup	toys on table and toys in a basket
sort	miscellaneous blocks with a pile of big and a pile of small and blocks left to be sorted
trace	a hand tracing around a circle shape
check your work	check mark

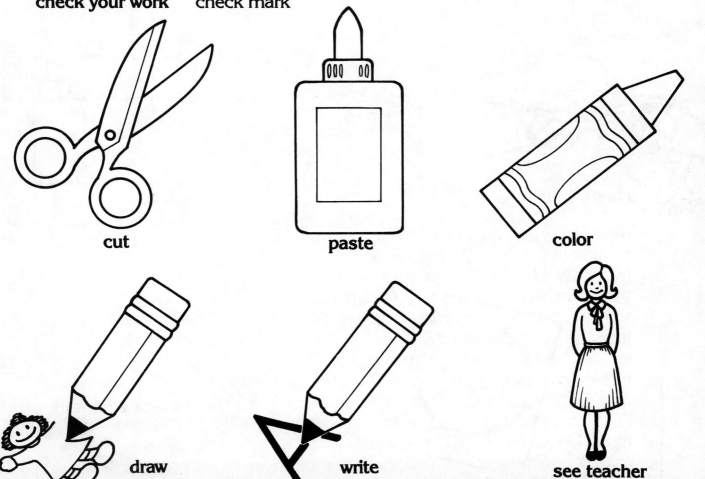

cut   paste   color

draw   write   see teacher

GA1093

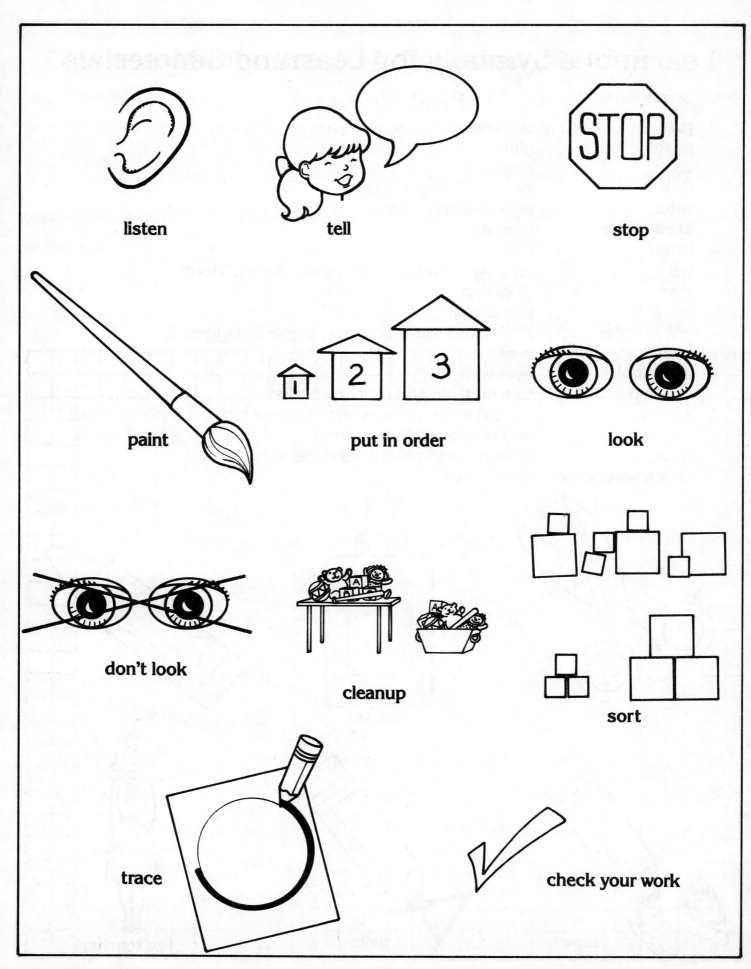

listen

tell

stop

paint

put in order

look

don't look

cleanup

sort

trace

check your work

GA1093

Learning Centers Using Classroom Materials

Bead Buddies

1. Bead buddies sit back-to-back. One person strings five beads.

2. The first person tells about his beads and the second person listens.

3. No looking.

4. Second person strings after listening.

5. Check your work. Now start again.

GA1093

Three-Way Puzzle

1. Do the puzzle in the frame.

2. Do the puzzle out of the frame.

3. Do the puzzle backwards.

50

GA1093

Creating an Environment

Two teachers can be given the exact same materials to teach, and yet each classroom will be unique and reflect the personality of the individual teacher and the children.

Some guidelines for setting up a classroom:

Children's Level: The classroom should operate at the children's level. If the children are young, then the posters, games, and supplies should be at a level where they can easily see and reach. Teachers should also sit on lower chairs when working with the group on the floor so that children are not looking up but looking straight ahead.

Visuals: Classrooms should not be stark or on visual overload but somewhere in between. Some children will become distracted if too many things are hanging from the ceiling and stuck to the walls. Classrooms should have a comfortable visual order that looks pleasant but not overdone.

Softness: Young children come from home environments with carpets, couches, pillows and blankets. Schools are filled with hard desks, chairs and cold floors. It is important that every classroom have a soft place which could be a rug, pillows or chairs. Children need to have a place where they can relax and be quiet if needed. Each individual knows how comforting it is to rest in a soft chair, and young children have those comfort needs on a very high level.

Things to Touch: Classrooms need interesting things for children to touch and explore every day. These things don't always need to tie in with the curriculum because exploration can be for exploration sake. Old telephones or anything with inside mechanisms are fascinating to children. Things from nature, like crystals and other items like musical instruments and kaleidoscopes, are fun.

Sound: Sound in a classroom can be an attraction or a distraction depending on how it is used. Some teachers and children have difficulty tolerating loud voices or outside distractions. Some teachers enjoy soft music playing in the background while children are working. If the music is instrumental and the teacher plays it often, it can become a psychological cue to begin work. There are children who are noise makers and are not content if things are too quiet and will make small noises. This may be part of their learning style. Be sensitive and yet move them from others they may distract.

If possible create a room that has available noisy spots and others where the expectation is to always be quiet, like the library area. If the room is located next to the main street or an active hallway, move the desks or tables so the children are not distracted by the outside activities.

Order, Disorder, Clutter: Each teacher has his/her own personal neatness code. Some teachers need a great deal of order in their lives and are unhappy without organization while others feel hemmed in if things are too orderly. The important thing to remember is that your classroom is also teaching children about order in their lives. The expectation is that children will be responsible for helping keep order and maintain the classroom. High piles of clutter demonstrate to children that that type of organization is acceptable. Teaching a child organizational skills can be of benefit to the child and to the teacher. Overdone order and organization can also stifle children and make them feel uncomfortable in their environment. A balance is needed.

Material Distribution: Games and materials piled high on shelves will only overwhelm children, not encourage them to participate. The learning materials need to be attractive and limited. Don't put everything out at once. Don't overload an area with too many materials. This feeling of overload is comparable to a bargain basement sale where there are good things everywhere, but you don't know what to do or where to go first.

Setting Your Goals and Organizing Your Records

Every school year begins with anticipation of a new beginning, fresh ideas and exciting possibilities. Teachers fall asleep with butterflies the night before school just like children. Each share the desire to have a successful school year.

Teachers have the opportunity to prepare their year based on the experiences from previous years. As we plan for the coming year, we assess what worked in the past and what new innovations would work with the upcoming class. The goal-setting sheets are designed for collection of good ideas. These planning sheets can be kept in the lesson plan book. Ideas that develop during the year or ideas that say, maybe next year, can be collected and saved for reference.

In addition teachers enjoy preparing their records so that the schedules, lesson plans and particular detailed information is ready for the start of the year. The following formats will help with the organization and preparation for the school year that begins with the best of intentions becoming a reality.

GA1093

Goals for the Year

Curriculum Ideas	Refer to:	Center Ideas	Refer to:
Holiday Activities	**Refer to:**	**Art Activities**	**Refer to:**
Parent Involvement	**Refer to:**	**Classroom Materials**	**Refer to:**

GA1093

Unit Ideas

Unit Idea	Materials	Resources

Teaching Ideas:

Things to Collect

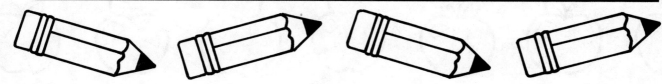

GA1093

Small Groups

Group:	Group:
Names:	**Names:**
Group:	**Group:**
Names:	**Names:**
Group:	**Group:**
Names:	**Names:**

GA1093

Money Collection

Activity

Student Names										
Totals										

GA1093

Bus Schedule and Assignments

Bus:	Time:	Bus:	Time:

Bus:	Time:	Bus:	Time:

GA1093

Transportation to and from School

Walkers
_____
_____
_____
_____
_____
_____

Riders
_____
_____
_____
_____
_____
_____

Other
_____
_____
_____
_____
_____

GA1093

Calendars, Attendance and Helper Boards
Calendars

Use tempera paint to paint the squares on the chalkboard for a chalkboard calendar. This saves valuable bulletin board space in some classrooms, and the numbers for each day are held with magnetic tape.

If a magnetic board is used, then special days can be noted with cute magnetic characters or shapes.

Create a pattern on your calendar with different objects like hearts and flowers and create a pattern of hearts, flowers, hearts, flowers. The children have to guess the new day's number and symbol.

Sun.	Mon.	Tues.	Wed.	Thurs.	Fri.	Sat.
			1	2	3	4
5	6	7	8	9	10	11
12	13	14	15	16	17	18
19	20	21	22	23	24	25
26	27	28				

Attendance

Attendance time can be used as a teaching time.

Children can check themselves in with a name card.

Children can recite their names, addresses or phone numbers when their names are called.

Children can count the number of boys, girls, and total each day.

Backwards attendance is when the class determines who is missing before the roll is called.

GA1093

Helpers, Helpers, Helpers

messenger

calendar keeper

flag holder

window monitor

sink monitor

chair monitor

desk/table monitor

art custodian

brush cleaner

book monitor

plant feeder

attendance taker

lights and doors keeper

coatroom watchdog

chair monitor

scissors dispenser

paper collector

mailperson

cleaners

paper supplier

ball monitor

equipment keeper

pencil sharpener

chalkboard monitor

wastebasket monitor

game monitor

class friend

nurse

staple user

hole puncher

snack server

boots monitor

teacher's desk helper

paper passer

This list gives the teacher the option to give everyone in the class a job. The job could be held for a week or even two weeks. This gives the child a chance to find out the responsibilities that are required with the job and a chance to meet those responsibilities over a longer time period.

The responsibilities for each job need to be clearly defined. The old helpers can teach the new helpers the responsibilities when they change jobs.

GA1093

62

Through the Eyes of a Child

The night before the first day of school my stomach churns and I feel nervous. I'm afraid I will oversleep and not wake up in time to get to school. I wonder who will be in my class and how the day will go. I can't believe another year is about to start.

Children and teachers share these thoughts as the school year is about to begin. It is enveloped in anticipation, excitement and optimism about the upcoming year. The success of that first hour and first day are important to the children and to the teacher. The schedule and routines that are established will be essential for classroom order. These next sections will share some techniques for the procedures and activities related to an early childhood classroom.

Orientation Schedules

Everyone wants their children to get off to a great start, and part of that success rests on the children's awareness of their new situation. School orientations have a host of variations, but the purpose remains that children and parents need to familiarize themselves with the new school situation.

Old Class—New Class Orientation

Invite the new or upcoming class to an end-of-the-year activity with the old class. This could be the end-of-the-year Teddy Bear Picnic or a field trip. Stay away from traditional classroom activities because the children may be concerned that school is too difficult because they are seeing the end-of-the-year progress. The old class can share routines such as bathroom, coats, lines and snack procedures.

63

Parents and Children Orientation

Invite the children and their parents for a short classroom orientation. This is best done in a staggered manner and allow no more than 5 to 10 parent-child groups at a time. Have an information form for the parents to fill out so the teacher can spend some time with the children showing them where to find their lockers or hooks, the bathroom and possibly read a story.

Shortened Class Day

Many teachers like an orientation with their entire class for a shortened class time period. During this time the teachers do some fun activities and go over the procedures that need to be followed. This shortened time period gives the children a chance to adjust to their new surroundings, separate from the parents and have a fun experience.

Evening Orientation

This is on the same level as an Open House where the family are welcomed to the school to meet the teachers and see the classroom. If certain areas or procedures are to be pointed out to the child, the responsibility will need to be explained to the parents. A letter like the following could be sent home prior to the evening or handed out at the door. The teacher can have a sticker, name tag or activity page that is to be returned the first day of school.

Orientation

Time:

Place:

Date:

We are so glad you are joining us for the early childhood orientation. While visiting our classroom, please point out the following areas to your child and help him/her get familiar with the area:

Help your child find his mailbox.

Help your child find his coat hook.

Discuss the bathroom and proper bathroom procedures of flushing and hand washing and drying.

Play with a puzzle or toy and remember to put the toy back where it belongs.

Remember to come up to your teacher and say "hello." She has something special waiting just for you. We all look forward to seeing you this evening.

Sincerely,

First-Day Survival Kit

First Hour

Organization is the key to a successful first hour and first day in the early childhood classroom. Teachers will have very little time to do anything but attend to the children and their needs and begin the process of acclimating them to their environment.

Getting Through the Classroom Door

Every school has its own policy about the children entering the building and coming into the classroom. The teacher should allow only the classroom children to enter the room starting on the first day. Many times parents and older siblings want to join the children. Although this may comfort some children, it causes confusion and anxiety for the children that are alone. The first rule should be—all good-byes at the classroom door. The teacher should be at the classroom door greeting the children.

Children Who Will Not Enter the Classroom

Every year there are children who will not enter the classroom and have a difficult time with separation. This is where the first rule will be broken. The easiest way to handle this is not to force the separation. If that option is not available, then the teacher will need to carefully draw the child into the room. Be careful not to become part of a tug-of-war. These scenes can become upsetting for everyone within earshot. Always put the child's safety first. If he/she makes a dart for the door, then physical intervention may be necessary. As quickly as possible attempt to get help from a volunteer or administrator. The teacher is responsible for the child. The child should not be left alone or with a helper due to liabilities. But a helper can stay with the child in the classroom and help make the adjustment easier.

GA1093

Everybody's Here—Let's Get Started

If children have had an orientation to school, they will be anxious to find the place for their coats and book bags. If they have never seen the environment, then the group needs to join together on the floor or at the tables to share what will come next. Have the volunteer show the children where to hang up their materials in small groups while the teacher starts off with a story or rhyme.

Attendance Ideas

- Use a chart where every child turns his name as he enters the room.
- When I call your name, sit down.
- Use a chart with each child's name printed and point to the chart as you call the attendance.

Who Has a Note?

The beginning of the year is always a time for communication with home, and the children are always carrying messages, forms and money. A routine should be established from the first day. The teacher could have a message box which is nothing more than a box with a large opening that has attractive wrapping. All messages go in the box as soon as the children enter.

Teachers working with young children may choose to use safety pins to pin on messages and receive messages back. This is a great system for important messages that need to be seen immediately by the teacher. A note to parents at the beginning of the year will help keep this system going.

Using the Bathroom

First things first. Teach a lesson about using the bathroom. This is where a few volunteers are necessary. Send the children in small groups and demonstrate how to flush, wash hands and throw away paper towels. Small children may have difficulty getting undressed and dressed. Parents should be encouraged to dress children in clothes that they can zip and snap.

If the bathroom is not near the classroom, then discuss with the children landmarks along the way to find its location next time. The class may go to the bathroom as a group, but every child should be able to find the bathroom by himself if necessary. The children should also know what conduct is expected going to and coming from the bathroom.

● ● ● ● ● ● ● ● ● ● ● ●

GA1093

When Are We Going to Have Fun?

Children come to school to have fun and to learn. They have been waiting and are anxious to play in the classroom environment and enjoy the new company. The classroom should be set up with the basic equipment, and the children should be allowed to play with the classroom materials. Review the rules of cleaning up and replacing toys and then let them explore their new environment.

During this time the teacher should keep moving throughout the room encouraging shy children and keeping a lid on the not-so-shy. The volunteers can be put to use in areas where the children may need more direction. This is the best time for the teacher to take note of the children and their adjustment to the school setting.

Cleanup

Teachers are masters of making mental notes of who played with what so that when it is time to clean up the teacher knows who left the toy in the middle of the room. Every child needs to be made responsible to clean to the best of his/her capability. Don't be dismayed if cleanup takes as much time as playtime. Cleaning is part of the lesson.

Quiet Time

Pacing from active to passive is essential in the early childhood classroom, and most active times should be followed by quiet times. This is best done with stories, rhymes, songs, finger plays, and jingles.

Theme Song: "It's the First Day of School" sung to "How Much Is That Doggie in the Window?"

Ho, Ho it's the first day of school.
My teacher and new friends are nice.
I like to come to this school.
Where learning is fun all the time.

Ho, Ho it's the first day of school.
My teacher and new friends are nice.
This is our new friend _____.
Welcome to _____ school.

Depending on the time available, you can sing verses one and two or just verse one or two. Instead of first day of school, the time can be changed to first week or first month.

GA1093

Helpers

Getting a few good helpers is essential to keeping the room organized during the first day of school. Helpers can do the following activities so the teacher can remain with the group:

- Attend to a nervous or sick child
- Take care of messages and notes
- Take milk or lunch count
- Help with bathroom routine
- Help with coat and book bag management
- Help supervise during playtime
- Read to a small group
- Help the teacher with organization and passing out of materials
- And much, much more

Raise Your Hand

What would school be without raising your hand? Young children who have not had previous school experience need to be taught this time-honored method of recognition. Here are some tricks to encourage a raised hand before a raised voice.

- Praise with a sticker or stamp on the hand of children who raise their hands before speaking.
- When the teacher asks the group a question, she should raise her own hand to indicate to the children that a raised hand is expected.
- Verbally praise the children who remember to raise their hands.
- Let everyone talk at once and ask the class to share answers with one another. Children quickly learn that they need to take turns and speak at the appropriate time.

GA1093

The Final Hour—"I Want to Go Home."

"When can I go home?" is a common question asked by many children in the month of September. For some children it is a long day or half day, and they feel as if it's taking forever to end. One reason for this is that the environment and classmates are strange and new. With no routines mastered, nothing familiar and many strange faces, the natural instinct is to return to what is known. As school and new friends become more familiar, the questions about going home lessen. The best transition for children is time. But in the meantime it is important for the teacher to keep the children assured that the end is coming and that they will return home today and return to school tomorrow. Here are some ideas that will hold them.

Puppet Magic

Every child sees something magical in a puppet. The puppet could be an animal or a character. The puppet might be anxious about being in school, and the teacher can ask the puppet questions that require a nod of the head or a shake. This way the teacher who is uncomfortable being a ventriloquist can talk to the character. The teacher can encourage the children to ask questions, and the puppet can whisper answers in the teacher's ear. The puppet can also whisper answers in the children's ears and the results can be charming.

The puppet can also take part in some jingles. Use any puppet and give it a name with character.

Ricky Rabbit, Ricky Rabbit,
What do you see?
I see _____ (child's name)
Smiling at me.

Buzzy Bear, Buzzy Bear,
What do you do?
I give hugs to
Kids like you!

GA1093

Let's Eat and Learn

Give the children stick and circle pretzels and eat your way through letters, numbers, terms like *half* and *whole* and *bigger* and *smaller*.

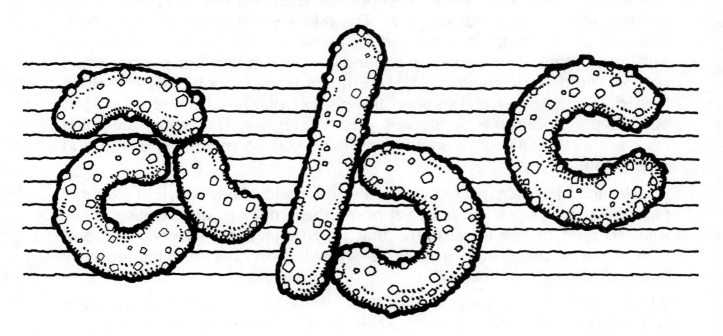

Special Stories

Have the children lie quietly on the floor and turn off the lights. Play music that is only instrumental and is quiet and peaceful. As the music begins to play, make up a story with the mood of the music. Have the children close their eyes and imagine the mental pictures. Here's an example.

Two children named Brian and Katie were walking home from school and it started to rain. At first the rain felt soft on their faces, but soon it started to rain harder and harder and it stung their cheeks. Brian and Katie were not afraid, but they knew that they needed to run for cover in a nearby bush. It was a big bush, and they could run inside the bushes and not get rained on. As they hid under the bush they laughed and were glad that they were together. They had been friends all their lives and had grown up next door to each other. This was another adventure for two best friends. Suddenly they heard a noise at their feet and they both jumped and bumped heads. Their heads hurt as they rubbed them and looked at each other, and in an instant they knew there was an animal with them in the bushes. But they were so jammed together they could not quite see what it was.

Stop the record and turn on the lights. Let the children tell you what is in the bushes and what the children should do. Ask them to describe Brian and Katie and to describe the animal. When they are done, return to the music and the story.

GA1093

Katie and Brian moved carefully so they wouldn't bump heads again and squatted so they would be closer to the ground. They were afraid but curious to see what was in the bushes with them. Suddenly something small and furry jumped out and ran between Katie's feet. It was a very small puppy that was very wet and scared. The puppy smelled wet and jumped on both children with wet and muddy paws. The rain was letting up and they both scooped up the puppy and headed for home. As they were walking, a girl with an umbrella came running up and said that it was her puppy. It had run out the door when she had come home from school. Katie and Brian looked at each other and handed the girl her puppy. She was so glad to see the puppy and the puppy was glad to see her. The puppy snuggled his nose in the little girl's shoulder. "Thank you so much," she said and off she ran.

Katie and Brian were disappointed, late and muddy. They both had thoughts of keeping the puppy. As they ran home their mothers were waiting. They were so glad to see their moms that they hugged them very close and snuggled their noses in their mothers' shoulders and began to tell the story of their lost and found puppy.

At the conclusion of the story, ask the children to come up with any other animal that could have been in the bush and how the story could have changed.

The children might enjoy coloring a picture of the puppy or the children, or creating their own version of the story.

GA1093

Clay

Children enjoy playing with clay, and it can be a good end-of-the-day activity. Each child needs a small ball of clay and a small mat on which to work. Inexpensive place mats can be cut in half and work very well.

Make something round.
Make something flat.
Make a snake.
Make something long and short.
Make something skinny and fat.
Make something big and little.
Make something square.
Make something that is alive.
Make something that is up and down.
Make your favorite letter.
Make your favorite number.
The possibilities are endless.

Getting Ready to Go Home

Always leave ample time to prepare for going home. Keep a special place for all notes that need to be distributed. The children will need attention in getting their materials together. Rushed children make mistakes and feel insecure. If the children ride buses home, give each bus a leader who is holding a sign that signifies the bus color or number code.

While You Wait

If the children are waiting for buses or parents, there may be some spare time. This is difficult for children and brings on anxiety. Try some of these while-you-wait activities.

- Review the day's activities.
- Give a letter and ask for the next letter.
- Children, children, what do you say?
  What did you do in school today?
- I Spy.
- I like _____; I don't like _____.
- Tall as a _____; small as a _____.
- Count backwards from 10.
- Touch your toe, elbow, etc.
- Sing a familiar song.
- Clap, clap, snap, repeat.
- Listen and do—blink two times and touch your head.
- Say the days of the week.
- Say the months of the year.

GA1093

"What's in a Wink?"
Affective Ideas That Build Rapport

● ● ● ● ● ● ● ● ● ●

Through the Eyes of a Child

Do you remember being winked at? Do you remember how you felt? A wink between two people has a feeling of being private and special. When the right person winks, it can set your mind racing, speed up your heartbeat and make you feel pretty terrific. A little muscle control to close one eye can do all that! How much effort does it take to wink? How much time? With little effort and little time, someone can make your day. We can do the same for the children in our classroom with a little effort and a little time by sending private messages in quiet ways that say to the children, "You're terrific."

Here are some ideas that will help build rapport in your classroom and in some cases turn behavior problems around, build self-esteem, settle nerves and show you care.

● As the children enter and leave your room, greet them by name and share something positive. You may not get every child every day, but they will look for your face at the door and share a personal moment.

● When a child does something very well and needs a reward, allow him to look through a kaleidoscope. This tells the child that it is positive to look at the world and see beautiful things. In this same vein, allow children to shake a beautiful snowball scene or ring the wind chimes. Bringing beautiful sights and sounds into your classroom shows you share an appreciation for the environment.

GA1093

- Share a joke with a child. Instead of putting a sticker on the paper, put it on the end of the child's nose. Make a funny face at someone. Don't be afraid of losing control at the price of being too serious. Have fun with your class.

- Get engaged with the activities. Take the time to play with the clay yourself while children are playing and promote discussions. Sit down on the floor and work on puzzles. Take your turn at the easel and paint a picture. When you sit among a group of children, they should accept you and not see you as an outsider but rather someone who also came to learn.

- Hold hands with everyone as much as possible.

- Treat children with the same respect you want from them. Say "please" and "thank you" when a common activity is done. Ask them rather than tell them. Allow them to make choices. Talk to them in a simple, clear and respectful manner.

- Look directly into each child's eyes and make contact. Listen to what they have to say and respect their opinions. Ask permission, or ask a child if he/she would like a hug. Don't be afraid to shed a tear with a child.

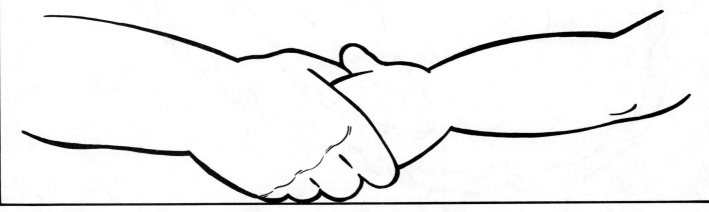

GA1093

- When a child is having a specific problem that needs daily reminders to break the habit, develop a signal that is only between you both. Every time the child falls back into old patterns a quiet reminder is just a signal away.

- Make eye contact—and smile!

- Tell children about personal stories from your life.

- Scratch a back on occasion.

- Give a pat on occasion.

- When a tragedy happens in your room, let the children discuss the situation and ask questions. Don't hide from the situation. The teacher's lack of discussion can signal real fear in some children, telling them this is something from which they should hide and be afraid.

- Ask yourself at the end of every day, "What did they teach ME today?" If you look, there will be a lesson.

- Communicate successes with parents by sending home happy grams that tell of today's bright spot.

- Create a class joke. Even little folks get the joke if repeated enough times. It could be a funny saying or an exaggerated word that always gets a reaction.

- Give me five—Children love to express their successes with the same actions that are common in their home setting or neighborhood.

- Swing on the swing, go down the slide, jump the jump rope and hop on the hopscotch.

- Don't forget to give a wink or a blink.

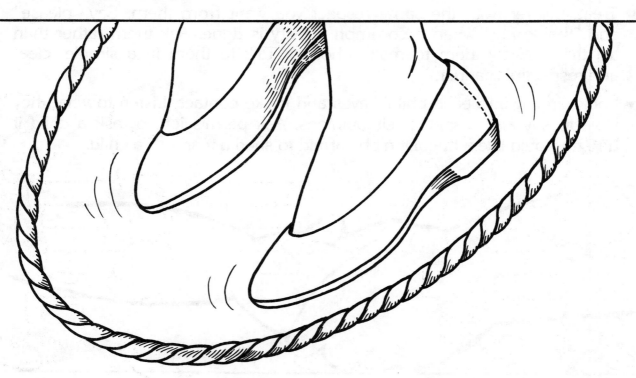

Routines

Routines are an intregal part of any classroom setting. The routines that are established give each classroom its own sense of community. Each structure that is repeated and followed daily gives children the sense of knowing what will come next. Routines relate feelings of security that help each child participate and give him/her a sense of belonging.

Every substitute teacher knows the stir that will be created when he or she violates the class routine. Children depend on that structure. Routines anchor their behaviors and give format to their day.

Line Up

When working with young children, it's always best to ask them to line up in small groups. Young children have a tendency to stampede for placement at the door. Here are some suggestions to line up by.

- table name
- hair color
- shoe style (Velcro, tie)
- boy/girl
- color of clothes
- eye color
- initial in first or last name
- number of letters in their first or last name
- number of brothers and sisters
- mode of transportation to school

Other Ideas:

- Say their addresses as they walk to the door
- Say their phone numbers as they walk to the door
- Count to 10 as they walk to the door

GA1093

Teacher's Name

Children should be encouraged to refer to their teacher by name. A simple technique is to repeat your name every time you are referred to as "teacher." Wait for the child to repeat your name before answering the question or meeting the need. This same technique can be used for "please" and "thank you."

As the teacher, make sure you express gratitude and expression of polite behavior to your children. When you step in a child's way, excuse yourself and when they fetch a staple gun, say "thank you." The lessons that are modeled by the teacher will be adopted by the children.

Story Time

Preparation is everything to a quality story time. As your group of children approaches for story time, separate children who have difficulty sitting next to each other and cause each other to be distracted. Have the children get comfortable but insist that their hands be in their own laps.

Before reading, ask a question that they can refer to while listening. Or, start with a brief discussion. Occasionally a prop makes an exciting start to story time.

Try to read and display the pictures simultaneously. If this is impossible, give lots of time for viewing the pictures. Reading and then showing takes more time and will be more difficult for children with short attention spans.

Read the story to yourself, and if two or three characters appear, try to change your vocal inflection. Read softly and then loudly. Read fast and slow. Read with love for the story. Read the stories you enjoy reading!

At the conclusion of the story always review.
- Make reference to other situations that tie into the children's lives. Have you ever had this feeling? How would you like that to happen to you? Have you ever been anywhere like it was in the story? What would you do?

- Ask the children to summarize the story with first, middle and end.

Show and Tell

Show and tell has a purpose: to get children up in front of their peers to talk. It should build confidence and promote self-worth. It's easy to lose sight of these goals after the same toy truck is mumbled over week after week, or when children begin a game called Can You Top This.

Here are some alternatives that can spark up your show and tell.

- Tell Only: Children are asked to tell about something in their lives.

- Color Show and Tell: Bring in something for each color, one color per week.

- I'm Special: Each child is assigned a day that is designated as his day. He shows and tells with pictures of his family or a visit from his grandparent or family pet. That day the child is the line leader and is given special jobs and responsibilities.

- 20 Questions Show and Tell: The children bring their show and tell in a bag and the class has 20 questions to guess what is in the bag.

- fall things   cyclinder things
  funny things   safety things
  hairy things   loveable things
  round things   square things
  things that open metal things
  The list can go on and on and on . . . .

                    GA1093

Starts and Stops and in Between

Starts

The beginning mood leading into a lesson or activity can frequently determine the success or failure of that lesson. The essential elements to a good beginning are the lead-in to the lesson, the ability to convey the expectations and the classroom chemistry.

Terrific Lead-Ins! (This Hooks Them)

Stories   Manipulative
Finger Plays   Puppet
Rhymes   Song
Something in a Magic Box   Food
Hat   Something Living
Tool   Picture
Personal Recollection   Joke

Laying Out the Expectation (This Directs Them)

When an activity is to take place that will require the children to follow directions, here are some key ideas to help the children remember the sequence of directions.

- Pretend you are the child and ask the class to teach you what should happen and how it should be done after you have taught the lesson.

- Use rebus symbols to order the sequence of a particular set of steps. This is a fun little song to teach that helps children remember the order for color, cut and then paste.

"Color, Cut and Paste" sung to "The Eensy Weensy Spider"

First we like to color
Color nice and bright.
Then we use our scissors
and cut with all our might.
Finally we paste and stick
it down real tight,
So we can smile and feel proud
that our work looks just right!

GA1093

Classroom Chemistry—(This Sets the Tone)

The room chemistry must be set by the teacher prior to each activity or lesson. It is a feeling conveyed that says to the children, this is serious, this is fun, this is important, this is joyful or whatever the message. This is done with the tone of the teacher's voice and the teacher's actions. If we convey through our voice and movements that this is important and that it is to be taken seriously, the children will follow that lead.

- Soft voice in a whisper says exciting or special.
- Loud voice says important or in control.
- Questioning voice says discovery or choice is involved.

Teachers weren't born with teacher voices; they develop their voices through years of working with children and learning the reaction that a particular voice elicits. This has to do, once again, with the art form of teaching and the need for each teacher to recognize her ability to set her own classroom chemistry.

Stops

Stops should be prepared for and led into gently. Stopping an activity requires change and many children have difficulty with the process of change. Here are some clues.

- On a large classroom clock, indicate the time the lesson will need to be completed. This allows the children to begin the personal awareness of time usage.

- As the activity continues, indicate to the children when half the time has been used and then give markers that tell when 10 minutes and 5 minutes are left to complete the activity.

- If children are not able to finish, then provide them with some options for completion. "Would you like to take this home and bring it back tomorrow or finish it here in class later this morning?"

- Some children never want to start, some never want to finish, and some are always done before others get started. Keeping children engaged in their work, interested and on task is one of the most difficult skills in teaching.

 GA1093

In Between

It's been said that young children can only work for short periods of time before they need a change. But many young children can work for an hour or more if the activity is interesting and engages their imagination. There should be no hard and fast rule about time limits, but rather the teacher should look at the tempo of the group and diagnose their needs as the teaching and activities flow. Here are some signs that will tell the teacher that the lesson is still on track.

The children are making eye contact.

The noise in the room is moderate.

Children are engaged in conversations that are related to the activities.

The children seem rooted and the level of movement is low.

Many of the children are very quiet and involved in the lesson.

As the lesson or activity continues, the pace and tempo will change. Children will begin to finish and will frequently disrupt the students who are engaged at a high level. One idea is to move students who are completed off to another activity that can be quickly cleaned up and is quiet.

The best solution is a visit to the room library where children can have a restful yet stimulating transition.

GA1093

The Pacing Is Off

Know when to quit! Sometimes a lesson is not getting across to a group of students. On occasion the teacher has not prepared the group or the appropriate materials and the order and pacing are gone as we hunt for the missing paper. Know when to start over! Don't be afraid to stop, regroup the students, quiet the room, stop the activity or begin the next day. There is no point in driving the train if you lose all the boxcars.

When the pacing is off, the children will show you with sure undeniable signs. The signs may be some of the following:

The children will show complete off-task behavior.

Most of the children seem to have no desire to complete the task or respond to the lesson.

The children seem lost and are all asking the same questions.

More children begin to show behavior problems.

The level of work completed is poor and not within the teacher's expectation.

Teachers need to do continuous evaluation and ask themselves what went wrong. Was the timing off (for example, had the children just done another similar activity)? Did the group just come in from playground and were too excited? Did I provide time to resettle? Did the lesson start with too much activity? Did I lose some of the children? Was it presented too fast or too slowly?

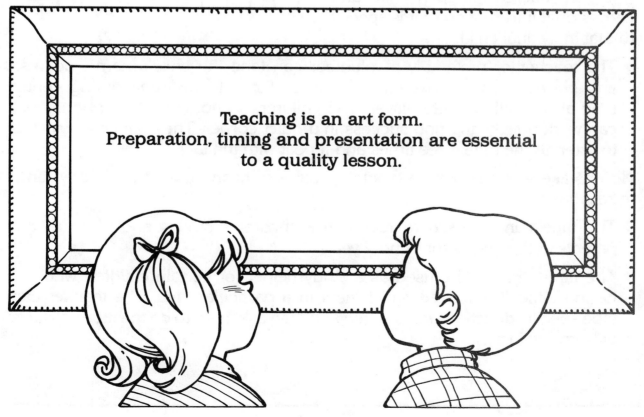

Teaching is an art form.
Preparation, timing and presentation are essential
to a quality lesson.

GA1093

Things We Need to Know
Learning Our Names

Many young children have not learned to pronounce their entire name using first and last names. Here is a song that gets children using their name.

"My Name Sounds Great" sung to "My Bonnie Lies over the Ocean"

My family gave me this name
It's special as special can be.
I like my name, it sounds great.
Listen, I'll tell you my name.

Susan Brown, Susan Brown, Susan Brown is my name, my name Darnita Plow, Darnita Plow, Darnita Plow is her name, her name.

Each child that gets identified gets to say his/her complete name or the children can pair up and share their names with other children.

My Personal Tape Center

Ask each child to bring in or contribute a blank audio cassette. These cassettes can be very inexpensive if bought at a discount. This cassette can be used for a variety of different activities throughout the year. It is personalized for each child and carries on it information that is special to that individual child.

- The teacher or preferably a volunteer can tape the child's name, address and phone number. The child can then listen to the tape during center time at a small cassette player. The children do not need headphones but can work quietly and find success in a quiet corner. They will be instructed to listen to the tape three times and repeat with the tape.

Note: Make sure the person taping speaks slowly and gives the children time to respond.

- The tape can be used to record the children's stories and given to the parents at the end of the school year.

- The tape can also be used as a study helper for certain children who are having difficulty or need enrichment in a particular area. The teacher can tape specific directions for children and then ask them to do the tape activities at home or in school.

GA1093

This Is Your Life

To stress the importance of a child's environment, each child can be chosen for a This Is Your Life day. A bulletin board area is devoted to the important statistics about each child. The house has a space for each child's house number and the street sign for the name of the street. The telephone will indicate the phone number, and the children the number of brothers and sisters. The grown-up will indicate the parents or guardians, and the child's name will be prominent across the top of the board.

Once again the teacher should find a volunteer to complete the writing for each child. When the child's day is over, the items are put in a book that is taken home when all the information is memorized.

Emergency Procedures

Every school has its own procedures for fire, tornado or earthquake drills. When working with young children, it is important to take some special steps to prepare the children for the drills. Many children will be convinced that the drill is actually the real event even with considerable preparation. Although adults look on drills as part of the process, children think of the reality of the actual event and frequently fear for their own safety.

- Define the word *drill.* Many children only know the word from the dentist. In this case a drill is a practice.

- Talk about making a plan. Children and adults are making a plan so if anything should happen, everyone will know what to do and where to go.

- Discuss the fact that they are a group that needs to stay together. It is important for them to stay with their group and not wander off alone.

- Being quiet is one of the hardest things for young children to understand because during exciting times or frightening times the first thing most people do is talk or yell. Instruct the children to LISTEN for instructions. In many real emergency situations people are so loud they cannot hear the necessary instructions to reach a safe destination.

- Reassure the children after the drill that they should feel safe because they have a plan and know what to do if an emergency should happen. Help them feel secure in knowing it is unlikely they will need their plan, but it is always good to have one.

GA1093

Learning Addresses and Phone Numbers

Children can learn a song and all the words on the radio or a commercial on television and yet have difficulty learning their addresses and phone numbers. If we borrow the idea of putting their addresses and phone numbers to jingles, children will have more success with sometimes complicated number and word patterns.

One quick rhyme to match the phone number with is the opening to

"<u>Yankee</u> <u>Doodle</u> <u>Went</u> <u>to</u> <u>Town</u>."
 3   5   1 · 0 9 8 5

Others: "Michael Rowed the Boat Ashore"
            "Twinkle, Twinkle, Little Star"
            "Jimmy Crack Corn (and I don't care)"
            "Old MacDonald Had a Farm"

Phone Number Bingo

Each child's phone number is written on a piece of long tagboard. The children are given chips, and they play just like Bingo only the winner is declared when all the numbers are called. This helps the children realize the numbers involved in their phone numbers and reinforces the visual with the auditory.

Zip Codes—Area Codes—and Emergency Numbers

Children need to also be aware of the additional codes that rule our systems. Even young children enjoy learning that people in other areas might have their same address, phone number or name and that the system of zip codes and area codes help the postmen and phone companies find each family's home.

GA1093

Address

Phone Number

Name

Teaching the Letters of the Alphabet

The job of teaching the letters is one that is enjoyed by many an early childhood teacher. Each letter is an adventure. We sing and chant and color and paste. We cook and share and dramatize and elaborate. Letters can be the greatest of fun to teach and to learn. And yet, even as we do the highest quality of activities, we still have children who don't remember the letters. They seem confused and lost in the process of letter identification. Let's look at some of the skills necessary to learn about the letter *H*.

1. The child must be able to visually discriminate the letter *H*. He must be able to SEE how that letter is different from the letter *K*. (visual)

2. The child must be able to HEAR the word *H* and connect that word *H* with the symbol *H*. (auditory)

3. The child must be able to put these skills together and consistently recall the letter *H* whenever it appears and have the ability to REPRODUCE the letter. (kinesthetic)

When you are assessing children's ability to identify letters, here are some simple steps that will help you to zoom in on where and how the child is processing.

1. Ask the child to find the letter that LOOKS like the one that you are holding in front of you. You display the letter and the child points to that letter *H*. (visual)

2. Ask the child to POINT TO the letter *H* in a set with four other letters. If the child is able to do this, then you know that he does receptively know the name of the letter. No visual cues. (auditory)

3. Next ask the child to DRAW the letter *H* using a sand table or cornmeal box. (kinesthetic)

88

Developmentally Appropriate Activities to Help with the Teaching of Letters and Letter Sounds

If the children have difficulty, here are some extension activities that will build these developmental areas.

Teaching the Letters Visually

- Start with the simple shapes and lines. Have the children sort, match and reproduce from the visual example.

  Use shapes and lines that are found in all the letters. You can do this by starting with *A* and taking each shape found in the capital and small letters and moving to *Z*.

  It should look something like this:

- As you play with these shapes, provide everything BUT paper and pencil. Try toothpicks, beans, rice, cornmeal, buttons and even stick and circle pretzels that get eaten into shapes. Make the children anxious to use the pencils—they might even ask to use them.

  Take those shapes and begin to build the letters. As the architects of the letters, they will begin to see the difference in each of the buildings. For some children allowing enough time at this building stage is essential.

- Children need to see lots of models of the letters they need to learn. They need to see things they can trace, touch and turn. A fun game is to put out five uppercase *S*'s that are 3D and ask them to turn all of them to look like *S*'s. At this stage always keep a correct working model in sight.

- Ditto pages that say, "Find the one that is different and put an *X* " are fine AFTER you have had lots of experiences enjoying the shapes, the feel and the look of letters.

  •

GA1093

Through the Eyes of a Child

Do you remember a particular class in school where you had to learn the terms for many different things? It might have been geography, English or even physics. Some students are very good at remembering terms and definitions for abstract concepts, but for many children it is a difficult challenge. Learning the words or sounds for the letters and later learning the difference between an adverb and a pronoun and an adjective can be extremely difficult. Our school system demands that we be good at labeling and learning terms. Classes are filled with terminology for concepts, systems, beliefs, and objects. Teaching the letters of the alphabet is in reality teaching the first course in language terminology. It must be done with care.

Teaching the Letters—Receptive and Expressive

- There are two parts to sound letter identification. The first is the actual name of the letter and the second is the sound that the letter produces.

- Names of Objects and Symbols: If you have children who cannot learn the letter names, they may have an equal amount of difficulty with other labels in their environment. An easy check is to name some simple objects and ask them to point to the objects. Here are some examples: Point to your knee, your sleeve, the doorknob. If they can point to these types of words, then you know that the words are in their storehouse of words.

  The next check is to see if they can verbally recall the words with no clues. You say to the child, "Tell me the name for this." Words should be chosen that are appropriate for the age of the child such as *flag, goose, nest, stamp*. Most children will know the vocabulary receptively (point to) before they will be able to express and recall the word.

- The best example of this concept is with color words. Many young children can pick up a red crayon when being asked before they can verbalize, "This is a red crayon."

- If you have children who have an empty storehouse of words or talk a great deal but use only a limited number of words, it is important to introduce a large variety of words into their environment and reinforce that every word has a concept or object to which it's attached. Build on a word a day picking fun and unusual words such as *canary, detergent, envelope* and *experiment*. Everyone benefits from these types of activities.

GA1093

Through the Eyes of a Child

Imagine if we taught about community helpers in this manner:

"Boys and girls, I'd like to tell you about the policeman. This is his uniform and this is what he looks like. Can you all say *policeman*?"

"POLICEMAN!"

"Very good. After Christmas I will teach you what the policeman does every day. Now the mailperson. This is her uniform and this is what she looks like, and later on I will teach you what she does every day."

This method of teaching sounds pretty silly. It would seem that by January we might get very confused and not know our policeman from our mailperson. To a great extent, that is what happens when we first teach letter names and then letter sounds. Children need to feel, touch, see and hear about the letters and their jobs in order to truly understand their meanings. Disjointed information leads to disjointed processing for children.

Teaching the Letter Sounds
Auditory

Teaching the sound that goes with the letter is nothing more than learning about the responsibilities given to that letter. Putting the sound and letter together is not confusing for children; it's a way to hook the information together.

Ideas for Teaching the Sounds:

- The most successful methods for sound identification is repetition and integration. Children need lots of opportunities to hear the sounds and practice the sounds, and they must immediately see the sound in the context of words.

- One fun activity is for children in your room to be responsible for representing a particular letter. This is especially effective if the letter is the same as their first or last name. Children can wear the letter and be the keeper of the sound. When anyone forgets, he/she may go to the M keeper and ask to hear the sound. The M keeper, Marie, will be happy to share her sound.

- The second step is to put those sounds into words from the very start. The point is not to read but to see the relationship between objects (strawhat), the abstract symbols (H-A-T) and the connection, "Those letters say hat like this hat."

91

GA1093

Teaching the Letters in the Written Form
Kinesthetic

● ● ● ● ● ● ● ● ● ●

Through the Eyes of a Child

The beautiful handwork of a calligrapher takes extraordinary patience and control. The same for the lines of an illustrator or graphic artist. Many of us as adults wish that we could produce that kind of work, and often we hand people our "chicken scratch" with an apology. The development of handwriting for children might be compared to a "chicken scratch" writer becoming a professional calligrapher. That means a tremendous amount of concentration. It can be done, but it takes the combination of mental control and physical coordination. The brain must be willing to send messages to the hand, and the hand must be willing to accept and interpret. Quite a miraculous process!

● When you start the writing process, start in places that have minimum amounts of failure. If you can smear it away and try again and again, then failures don't stare back. Try these mediums: cornmeal or sand on the bottom of boxes, finger paint, magic slates, and chalkboards. These experiences allow for limited frustration and high levels of enthusiasm.

92

GA1093

Capturing the Letters

After lots of open-ended activities with various mediums, try capturing the image. This can be done with the lines and shapes that lead up to letter writing. Using paper, blot the images on the finger paint. (The letters themselves will appear backwards and may bring up some exciting experiences while looking in a mirror.) Don't be afraid to show children the wrong side of a 3D letter or its look in reverse as long as the correct model is there for the comparison.

- Before you write on paper, write in these places: in the air, on the palm of your hand, on your neighbor's back, on your thigh, on the bottom of your foot. You might even have Touchy, Tickle Letter Time. This may sound silly but it is serious business. Remarkable strides can be made by the touch process. Do this as much as possible.

- Writing within a confined space can be the most difficult element of writing for some children, so explain to them that one of the rules of writing is that it has to be within a given space.

- Start with writing a letter in one of the four boxes of a sheet of paper.

- Next, write the letter between two lines with a divider. Use an overhead so that the children can see the model.

- For some children this last step will take the longest. Seeing the lines, the spaces, the letter in its correct form and keeping it from being reversed can be overwhelming. Remember great calligraphy talent takes time, concentration and control.

None of these processes will insure anything. For some children the process must be broken down and observed, manipulated, developed and reinforced. Learning letters is an art form.

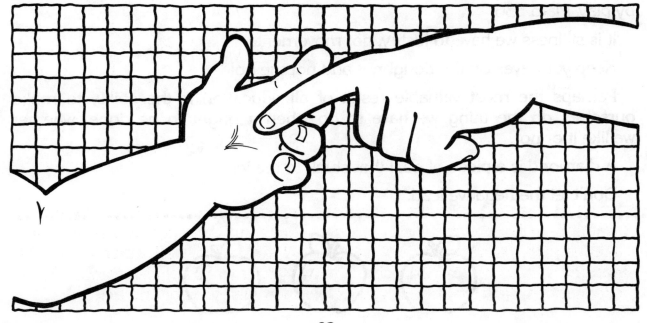

93

GA1093

Open House

The purpose of Open House is to give parents a feel for their child's school environment on a daily basis. Open House also gives teachers a chance to express their teaching philosophy and share the exciting activities and materials that are provided to stimulate learning. Finally, Open House is a time to display the child's work so the parents can get a perspective of the child's accomplishments.

Video Instruction

With today's access to video cameras, a simple Open House activity is to tape the class doing a variety of different activities from small group to whole group songs and possibly include playground activities, lunch or gym. This gives the parents a chance to see the children in action and gives a clear picture of the class in a variety of situations. It also helps the teacher dramatize the variety of situations and activities provided for in the classroom. When parents ask, "What did you do today?" they will know the children did more than "Nothing."

Teachers' Philosophy

Teachers dramatize their teaching style and their areas of interest in the organization and environment in the classroom. One technique for sharing your philosophy is to post quotes about teaching above the lockers or in your desk area. This says to those who choose to stop and read that these are some of your beliefs about teaching. (Below are some personal favorites. I'm sure you have some of your own.)

Do not, then my friend, keep children to their studies by compulsion but by play. Plato 536

It is stillness we have to justify, not movement.

Keep your eyes on the doughnut and not the hole.

Perhaps the most valuable result of all education is the ability to make ourselves do the thing we have to do when it ought to be done, whether we like it or not.

A diamond is a piece of coal that stuck to the job.

Don't let the negative lead.

GA1093

Open House Treasure Hunt

When parents enter a classroom, they frequently make one pass through the room and look in the child's desk, locker and mailbox and either get in line to talk to the teacher or leave the room. Our classroom environment has lots to teach parents, but they may not know what to look for or what they should touch.

Consider creating a ten-item search sheet that the parent completes with the child or alone as they visit the room. If the child is present, the clues can be stated in a way to help the child and parent unravel the riddle. For example: This is a place that has items that teach about words. Find the word *elder* and write the name of the elder in your group.

Other items might include asking the parents to visit all ten stations and complete a task at each station. For example: Math—create ten problems for your child to complete as seatwork tomorrow morning. Reading—please read this short story and draw a picture for your child. Science—match these pictures with these safety rules. Sandbox—find the two containers that hold the same volume of sand.

Talking with Parents

Parents are anxious to hear about the progress of their child, but Open House is not the place for a conference. Provide a sign-in sheet for parents who wish to sign up for a conference on a future date. When the parents and teacher meet, the teacher should make a positive remark about each child. Some teachers will say no conferences and then proceed to confer with the parent about the child's behavior or learning skills. It is important for the teacher to remark to the parents that a conference is requested. Always try to keep the tone of the Open House positive.

GA1093

Cooperative Learning Techniques for Little Folks

Cooperative learning techniques are designed to encourage positive interaction between children and shared responsibility for learning. These techniques need to be prefaced with teacher instruction and guidelines.

1. Think for yourself.
2. Share your answer.
3. Listen to the other person's answer.

Remember: Learning is a social experience. Observing children in these situations can give valuable information about language skills, leadership and creativity.

Roly-Poly Partners

Children are paired and sit foot-to-foot and hold hands. The children will rock back and forth and on each rock back an answer will be given.

- Children can recite the alphabet.
- They can recite a rhyme.
- They can name a color.
- Children can call out a number in sequence.
- They can recite a nursery rhyme.

This technique may take some practice, but the skills being taught include listening, motor coordination and skill development.

GA1093

That's My Answer

Children often don't listen to each other's answers during group discussion time. They frequently repeat an answer given by another child. When a specific set of responses is requested, play That's My Answer.

1. Ask a specific question such as "Think of a zoo animal."
2. Ask the children to think only of their answer and not to share it with anyone.
3. Picture your answer in your mind.
4. If you hear someone give your answer, you may stand up with that person.
5. Begin to ask for answers and record them on the board or chart.
6. At the conclusion, everyone should be standing and the teacher should have a list with no duplications.

Note: If a large group of children stand for one answer, ask them all to sit and think of some other answer that might be unusual or unique.

Best Buddies

In the game Best Buddies the object is to communicate and listen carefully. Children are paired and sit back-to-back. The children can have any sort of manipulative in front of them, but they must each have identical items such as inch cubes and the number of items should be limited.

1. The first child builds or puts the objects together in a simple way. The second child does not look.
2. The first child communicates to the second child how he/she put the objects. The second child is allowed to ask questions.
3. The second child builds or puts the objects together and shows the results to the first child.
4. The children then check each other's creation and the second child begins as the leader.

GA1093

Group Project

Children frequently enjoy doing a group project. They are set on the task and must work together as a group to finish the one larger project. Remember the original rules.

1. Think of your answer.
2. Share your answer.
3. Listen to the other person's answer.

This will become important as they begin to use various strategies to get the project done.

1. Large group dinosaur—The teacher can trace the outline or make large tracers and the children can decide how to color, paint or cut the dinosaur.

2. The clay castle—The children are all given clay that must be put together to create a castle.

3. Make a man—One child is traced by the others and the illustration is completed as a group.

4. Shape city—The children are encouraged to cut various shapes (use templates if necessary) and together glue the shapes together to create a shape city.

Areas of Group Discussion

- How did it feel when some people did not help in the group?
- How did it feel when some people had a hard time sharing?
- How did it feel when the project was all done?

GA1093

Children-Made Classroom Games

Work Smarter, Not Harder

"Boys and girls, I spent a great deal of time making this game for our classroom and now we are missing two parts. It makes Mrs. Anthony very sad when she cannot find the parts to the game after working so hard to make it nice for our classroom."

Sound familiar? It is human nature to be upset and disappointed when you spend four hours making a game and two pieces are suddenly missing the first week. Carefully pick the games you plan to make for your classroom. Spend your time wisely.

A better idea is to let the children make the games for your classroom. These classroom games can be used and abused and then thrown away at the end of the month or year with no hard feelings or long hours for the teacher.

Many of these games involve cooperative learning techniques. Have the children paired and working together or allow small group participation to create a class game. The children love the process and everyone enjoys the game. An added plus is that the game can be created during a class lesson. Any of these games can be laminated or used and discarded.

Here are some examples of how these games look and the approach used to involve your students.

Rub-a-Dub Leaf Matchup

Bring a variety of five different fall leaves that are still fresh. Rubber cement them to the table with the vein side up. Have the children, working in small groups, do leaf rubbings on lightweight paper using the side of their crayon. Have the child sign his/her name to the completed rubbing. After the children are done, the teacher cuts the edges of the paper on the paper cutter to square the papers and make them uniform. Then the teacher can mount them on heavier construction paper or tagboard.

This becomes a matching game where the children must find the rubbings that were done with the exact same leaf. The details will depend on your choice of leaves. You can choose from the same tree only different sizes or completely different trees. This is good for your children's visual discrimination skills.

99

GA1093

Rhyming Pumpkins

Have the children work in pairs. Give them old workbooks or magazines and send them on a mission to find two rhyming words. You may want to narrow the choices and run off some ditto pages that are likely to have rhyming pairs. Don't make this too easy or the value of the exploration will be lost.

Once the rhyming pair is found, the teacher checks their choices and they color their pictures if necessary. Each child is then asked to create his/her own pumpkin and glue the rhyming word to the front. So the game won't become too large, provide quarter-sized sheets of orange construction paper. These pumpkins may each look very different but each has a matching pair. These pumpkins all go in a basket and become the rhyming pumpkin game.

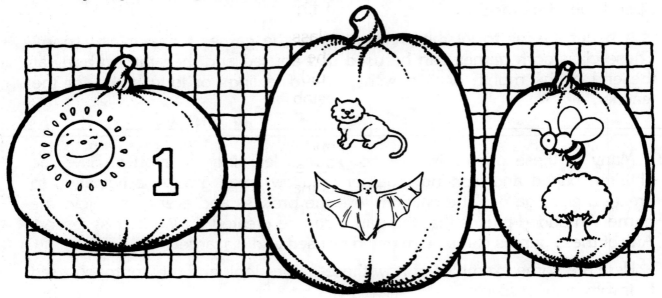

Turkey Dinner Alphabet Matchup

This game uses commercial illustrations of Pilgrims and Indians. The children color the Pilgrims and Indians and then place them on a large piece of paper suited to a narrow mural. It needs to be long enough to stand twenty-six of the characters side by side. Each character will be labeled A—Z. Shelf paper and backing paper cut down the middle work well for this game. The children will also color and cut a turkey shape, and the teacher will label each turkey with lowercase letters a—z.

Mark the characters with capital and lowercase letters prior to gluing them on the mural. A class lesson is created as the game is created. This game is especially enticing because it stretches across the floor.

The possibilities are endless. Children enjoy playing with their own work and seeing each other's ideas. Best of all, it creates more classroom teaching tools and saves the teacher time for other types of activities.

GA1093

Discipline

Discipline fits into this three-level framework: rules, choices and consequences. A portion of every teacher's paycheck includes the responsibility for discipline. It is an important part of every teacher's job. Some days and some years it seems to be a larger portion of the job than the teacher would like. In some cases children need the discipline so they can receive the education.

As teachers, our responsibility is to establish appropriate rules and reinforce those rules with appropriate consequences. The children's responsibility is to make choices about those rules.

Establishing the Rules

The rules that are established for the classroom should be fair, reasonable and within the range of expectation for the age of the child. The rules should be stated clearly for the children and should be limited enough so the children can recall the rules. The children can establish the rules and consequences as a class through discussion.

Each class has a tempo, noise level and organizational style. Each teacher must determine the rules within his/her environment. For example, some teachers might see loud conversation as inappropriate while others might be comfortable with a particular loud noise level.

Here are some samples.

- No throwing of toys.
- Walk in the halls.
- No pushing or shoving.
- If you play with something, put it away.
- Listen when the teacher is speaking.
- Keep your hands to yourself.

GA1093

Bumper Pad Discipline

Class Courtesies: Class courtesies are those daily, hourly and minute-to-minute classroom control issues. These behaviors are nurtured and taught through persistent reminders and guidance.

Quiet voices	Share
Push in your chair	Say "please" and "thank you"
Cooperate	Sit quietly
Take turns	Listen

A twenty-minute teaching lesson may contain ten comments by the teacher that continually monitor these behaviors. The teacher helps the children to stay within the parameters. Some children will make choices where they step outside the parameters of appropriate classroom behavior. The consequences are in place, and it is the teacher's discretion to level the discipline in line with the act.

Not every rule needs to be stated. If a child sticks out his foot and trips another child deliberately, common sense tells us that it is time to take action.

Consequences

Consequences should line up with the rule infraction as closely as possible. For example:

If a child is using a loud voice, he/she should be made to be quiet and isolated.

If a child throws a toy, he/she should lose toy-playing privileges.

If a child runs in the hall, he/she should be made to walk the hall.

The children should have the rules explained from the beginning of the year and have a clear understanding of why the rules are needed.

GA1093

The Teacher's Reaction to Behavior Problems

Teachers should not feel responsible for children's choices and uncomfortable with consequences. Don't take ownership for children's choices.

Discipline by the teacher should not include threats, anger, disgust, disdain or coercion. Some children may spend their entire year learning about making appropriate choices. Don't deny them the opportunity. It's far superior to learn about these rules, choices and consequences at a young age rather than later when the consequences become more serious.

How should a teacher respond to discipline? With indifference. Any response to the negative reinforces the very behavior you are attempting to stop!

"Joe, you made a choice to pinch David again today. That hurts David. You will need to sit out of play time today. I hope that tomorrow you will think about your choice."

Note: What was left out? Judgement! "That was a bad choice. I don't like the way you act. You make me very unhappy when you do that." Don't judge or respond with your feelings. Discuss the fact that it was a choice and the fact that the child will need to serve the consequences.

Why Not Discuss the Behavior Right There as It Happens?

When someone is scolding, we tend to do mental blocking and defend ourselves as the person is outlining all the things we've done wrong. Our defense system is in high gear.

When Do We Discuss the Behavior?

The behavior can be discussed before or after the actual incident takes place. Children can be reminded of the expectations and encouraged to cooperate, or they can discuss the behavior after the consequence has been served.

GA1093

This is obviously a simplified scenario. Teachers today face some extraordinary discipline problems in their classrooms. But those children with severe behavior are still making choices although they may not recognize that fact. It's a teacher's job to make the child aware that he has a CHOICE. There is a valuable lesson on either end of that choice. Your role is to facilitate EITHER lesson with fairness, reason and within the range of expectation. Bumper pad discipline continues throughout life, but the crib keeps getting bigger. Children expand from running in the halls to smoking in the lavatory to involvement with drugs to tax evasion. Each of us faces choices and each choice is followed by a consequence, positive or negative, and each consequence is followed by a LESSON. The lessons of life are part of the journey.

Quiet Voices

Take Turns

Push in Your Chair

Walk in the Halls

Keep Your Hands to Yourself

GA1093

Newsletters and Calendars

News from school is very important for parents and children. It gives the parents information they can share with the child, and it builds the necessary rapport between home and school.

Two formats are included as quick and easy tools for communication. The first is a newsletter format for each month. The newsletter can be informative and share the activities for the month. It can also include funny remarks made by children or interesting observations. It should be personal to the children in that room and the activities that are taking place.

The second is a calendar of monthly events. This can be used in two ways. The first is to send the calendar home at the beginning of the month and share important dates and suggest activities the parents might enjoy doing with their child. The second is to send the calendar home at the end of the month. Record activities completed, units taught and interesting classroom events. Parents will enjoy reading over the monthly events and will gain insight into the variety of information being taught in the classroom.

Teaching has become a solitary profession. We are alone in a room with children who when asked tell the world every day that we did "nothing." The general public and news media don't often share positive views of education, so the responsibility lies with each individual teacher to share his classroom with the outside world of parents and community and become an advocate for his teaching and the profession.

GA1093

September Newsletter

GA1093

October Newsletter

November Newsletter

GA1093

December Newsletter

January Newsletter

GA1093

February
Newsletter

GA1093

March Newsletter

April Newsletter

GA1093

May
Newsletter

GA1093

June
Newsletter

_____

_____

_____

_____

_____

_____

_____

_____

_____

_____

_____

_____

_____

_____

_____

_____

_____

_____

_____

_____

_____

_____

_____

_____

GA1093

September

October

GA1093

November

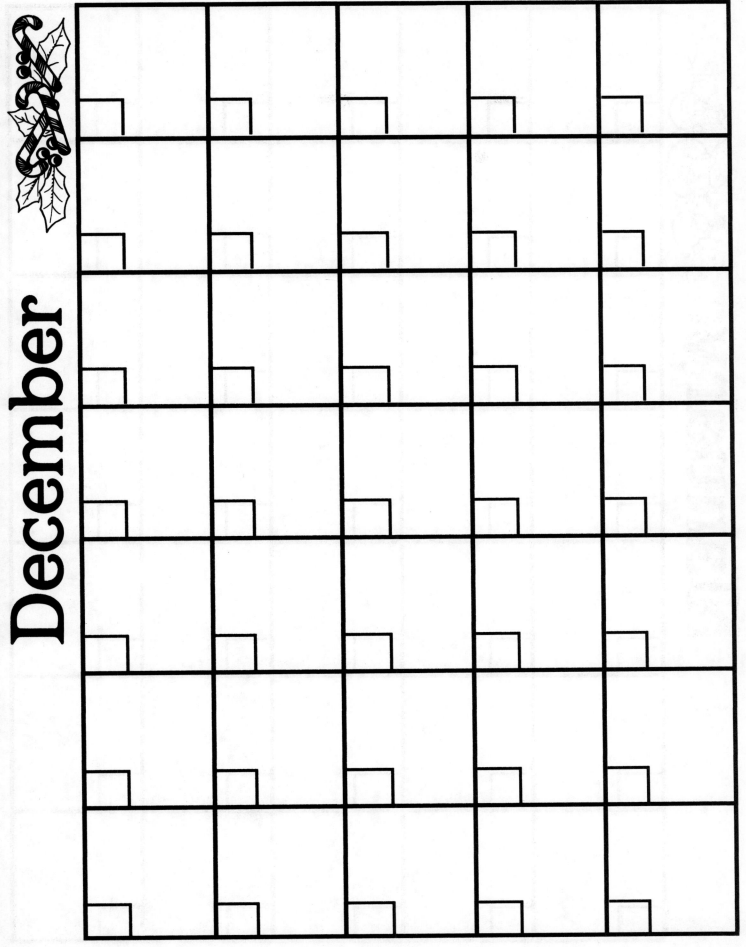

December

GA1093

January

GA1093

February

GA1093

March

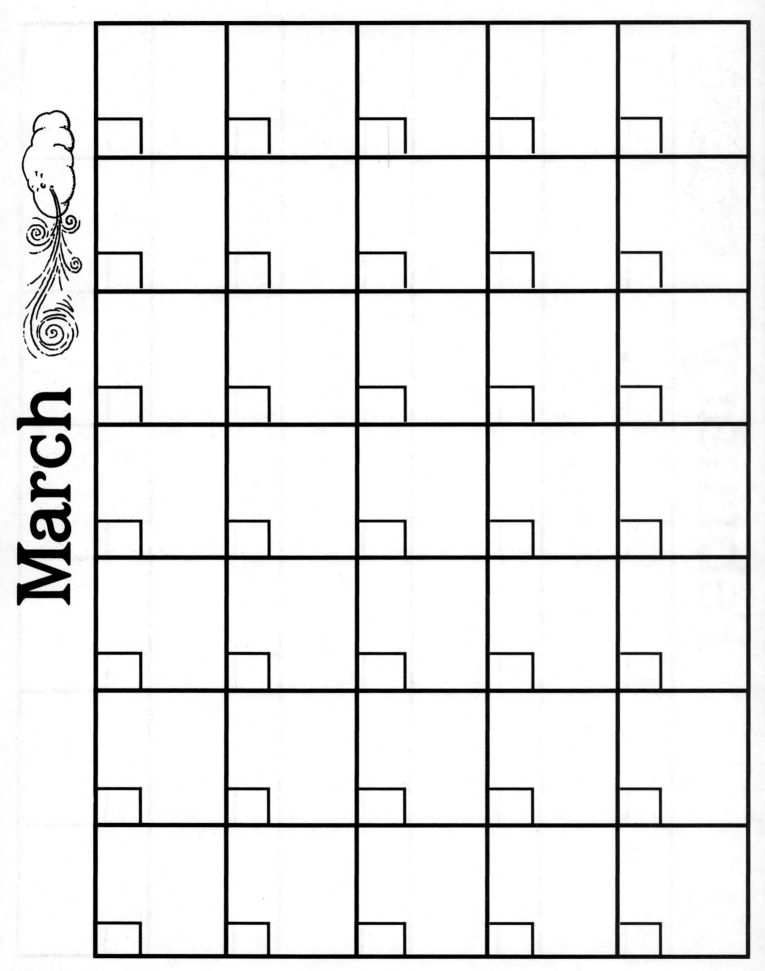

April

GA1093

May

GA1093

June

GA1093

Birthdays Are Something Special

Birthday Banners

Clay, a straw and a piece of paper make a cute little banner for every birthday child's desk. Commercially purchased suction cups also work. The banners may be done by a volunteer earlier in the year.

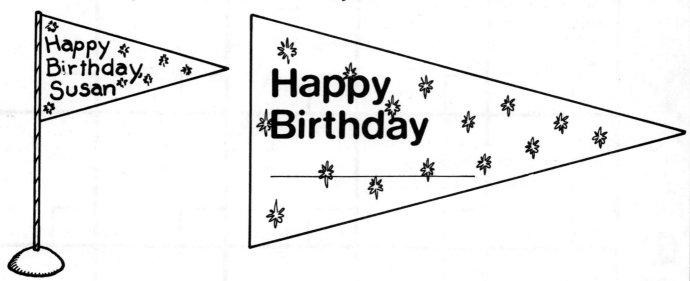

Birthday Buttons

Children love a personalized button for their birthday. Run the design on colored paper and have each individualized for each child by a volunteer. Laminate or cover with clear Con-Tact paper and have them cut and ready to go.

126

GA1093

Substitute Ideas

Substituting is said to be one of the toughest jobs in the field of education. An unknown classroom full of unknown children can be made more familiar with a little preparation by the classroom teacher. The following is a list of ideas to help the substitute feel welcome in your classroom.

- Indicate the location of your books and materials.

- Leave some hot chocolate or soup packets in your drawer for the sub who may have run out the door after a late call.

- Leave an audio tape of your morning exercises and songs with the words or book for the sub. Children dislike their routines changed, and this will help with the continuity.

- Leave a clear schedule of times and special activities. As a substitute one of the most difficult parts is pacing the lessons. Leave clear directions about the amount of time needed and when to start and stop.

- Keep a generic day's lesson with handouts, art project, movement activities and all the trimmings ready in a large envelope marked "substitute." This will be invaluable for the substitute and leave you worry free when illness or an emergency occurs.

- Ask the substitute to leave you a note about the day and the children's behavior.

- Leave the name of helpful children, aides and volunteers and other staff in the building.

- A list should be posted about all the little things like children with special needs, bus schedules, field trips or assemblies, attendance procedures, etc.

- Make sure the aspirin is in clear view.

If all of this is done well in advance, the emergency at home won't have to turn into an emergency at school.

GA1093

Volunteers

Through the Eyes of a Volunteer

Imagine a trained psychologist saying to you, "I have a few patients who need some extra help, and I'd like you to work with them. Just take them in the hall and do these activities with them."

Can you imagine yourself feeling very uncomfortable and thinking that this is not your profession and that you don't want to make any mistakes with these people?

Most teachers go to school for at least four years and many have post-graduate hours and master's degrees. As teachers, we have put a great deal of time and energy into our professions, and yet we expect novices to jump in with little or no preparation. A good volunteer program rests on the training and inservice given to the parents, community and students who will share the responsibility of working with our children.

Welcome Volunteers

Volunteers should be made to feel at home in the school environment. Here are some welcoming ideas.

- A notebook with written instructions for the day
- A place for coat and belongings
- A specific location for the day's duties and materials
- A consistent set of expectations

Volunteers as Workers

Many teachers and staff choose to use volunteers as helpers with clerical work and the time-consuming work of art project preparation, material duplication or paper correction.

This type of work needs very clear instructions and direction. Make sure you indicate exactly what you want to have done. Include a sample and take the time to explain in person. There is nothing more frustrating to both teacher and volunteer than a major project done wrong because of unclear or misunderstood directions.

Make a place for volunteers to work in the classroom and provide them with appropriate tools. It should appear that they were expected and prepared for before their arrival. Many times, having a volunteer means work on the part of the teacher, but the time invested will save more time in the future.

GA1093

Volunteers as Teachers

Volunteers that are involved with children in the classroom need to have some instruction before they begin working with the children.

Here are some possible topics of discussion.

- How to begin a lesson
- Expectations for the children
- Learning styles of the particular children
- Goals of the instruction
- How to handle discipline problems
- Ideas for expanding on a lesson once the initial concept is taught
- Time limits
- Lesson closure
- Notes of communication on children's progress

Let's Say "Thanks"

Volunteers need to be consistently reminded that their contribution is recognized and appreciated. This is extremely important and doesn't need to be an overwhelming project.

- Use happy grams.
- Encourage children to say "thank you."
- Tell the volunteer how much the children look forward to his/her visit.
- Remember the volunteer during the holidays.
- Praise the volunteer and the progress of the children.

GA1093

For Our "Sunsational" Volunteer

_____
_____
_____
_____
_____
_____
_____

• • • • • • • • • • •

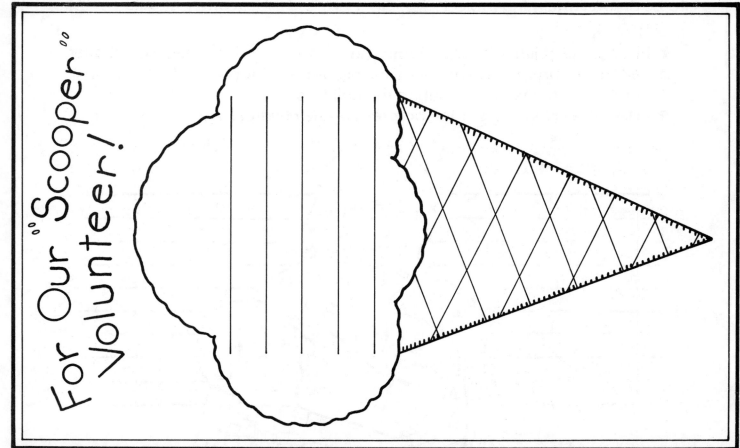

For Our "Scooper" Volunteer!

130

GA1093

How to Overcome the Snags of a Volunteer Program

No Shows

One of the snags in a volunteer program is that people may have other responsibilities or have difficulty keeping the commitment. A volunteer organizer helps keep the classroom continuity. Teachers grow to depend on the volunteer and plan their activities around that person's help. A volunteer organizer can be someone who does not go into the school but is willing to find substitutes for absent volunteers and keep the program going.

The expectation for reliability on the part of the volunteer should be discussed from the very beginning. The person needs to know that he/she is playing an important and valuable part in the daily workings of the classroom and that the success of the program lies in his/her participation. The organizer can help with emergency situations and find temporary fill-ins for the volunteer.

Classroom Privacy

The issue of confidential information needs to be discussed with all volunteers. Every parent has had the painful experience of hearing something negative about his/her child from a neighbor or family member. It's hard to listen to negative comments about our children because of our love and the reflection it makes on our role as parents. These comments should not be coming from a classroom volunteer to another parent or to anyone outside the classroom situation.

If this issue of privacy is discussed from the beginning in a serious manner, there is less chance of an incident occurring in the future.

Not Everyone Fits Every Situation

Occasionally a volunteer will not fit with the children or does not work well in the classroom situation. The teacher must maintain the right to make the final decision about the volunteer. The needs of the children are the first priority and responsibility. If their needs are not being met, then the teacher needs to make the necessary changes. This is not an easy decision or situation, but it can and should be handled with kindness and sensitivity.

                     GA1093

Joey

Joey was a sunny child who entered my classroom with a smile that crookedly crossed his face and shone in his eyes. Joey had a physical impairment caused during surgery. One side of Joey's face was paralyzed. One side of his face was that of any child and the other side from brow to chin was misshapen. Joey had limited control on the left side of his face and normal control on the right side.

Joey and that class of children made that the most rewarding year in my career. There was a community in the classroom that year. The incidents of questions came from parents, not from children. We all hugged a lot that year, and Joey got his share from me and from his peers. Becky, a beautiful ray of sunshine, became "Joey's girl." One day while I was reading I saw Becky lean over and kiss Joey's left side.

Every teaching career will have its Joey. The relationships reach far deeper than identification and remediation and touch us, change us and forever remain dear to our hearts.

Early childhood teachers are frequently the first professional to recognize a problem with a child. Years of teaching young children give teachers the tools to be diagnosticians. You learn the warning signs, the abnormal behaviors or the gut-level feelings.

Many teachers of young children are in situations where children with special needs are placed in their classrooms because of lack of alternate facilities. Teachers with little background in working with special needs children may not know where to start or how to identify or isolate the problem.

This next section is a resource of ideas on working with speech and language problems, English as a second language (ESL), hearing impairments, visual impairments and educationally handicapped students.

Early Childhood Teachers Need:
- to know the developmental characteristics of the children they teach
- to be observers and make time daily to observe children
- to build good rapport with parents and understand children's backgrounds
- to look at each child as an individual with strengths and areas of need
- to recognize that the teacher may be the person who will first identify children's needs and signal for help with resource personnel

GA1093

Speech and Language

Talking falls into two areas. One is the actual physical act of sound reproduction and the second is functional language that allows children to communicate their ideas and needs. Talking is our primary means of communication and it is essential.

Articulation

Problems with articulation can be corrected with the highest percentage of success. Young children are usually receptive to treatment. Typical problems include *omissions* of a beginning, middle or ending consonant sound. *Substitutions* consistently produce an alternate sound for a particular consonant. *Distortions* are poor formation or production of a particular sound. In general, consonants create more problems than vowels.

Causes

The consonant sound is created by obstructing a free air passage with lips, teeth or tongue. The muscles and dental structures may be part of the problem. Other causes may be poor models or physical development. Children who suffer from chronic ear infections may also have distorted reproduction. Note that school hearing tests and routine checkups may not catch hearing impairment in children.

Language Development

Language problems may be identified by noting some of the following areas:
- Does the child demonstrate diversity in his/her language patterns?
- Is the pitch, volume and tone within the parameters of normal?
- Does the child speak at a normal rate of speed?
- Is the speech in the range of maturity expected for that age or demonstrated within that community?
- Does the child generate language independently?

Classroom Interventions

- Alphabet cards with the photograph of the modeled speech sound being produced can be used with the whole class but emphasized to those children with problems.
- The teacher can reinforce specific behaviors after a visit to the speech clinician.
- The teacher can offer support and communication with the parents.
- The teacher can offer the child a correct model of speech sounds and language.
- A mirror can be made available for the children to watch their speech.

GA1093

Cultural Language

In some classrooms cultural speech patterns may be evident. Criticism of these may confuse children and poorly affect their self-esteem. Teachers should look at the substance of the communication and the richness of the content rather than the language structure. Teachers should model traditional speech patterns and encourage children with sensitivity.

English as a Second Language (ESL)

When English is taught in a classroom, it should be presented as enriching rather than restrictive. Children should feel that it is a positive and fun experience rather than one that limits their abilities for communication. English is our native language and should be taught with the same respect given to the child's native language.

In classrooms with ESL children, the environment should be language rich. Listed below are ideas to enhance your classroom for language.

- Listening centers with taped words that are repeated by the child and picture flip cards that correlate with the taped words should be available.
- Speech modeling should be sensitive to tone, pace, enunciation and articulation.
- Verbally label everything in the child's path and encourage all the children to continually use words and gestures to help the ESL children.
- Model listening to the ESL child and make every attempt to understand their needs. This active listening will be a model for the child when it is his turn to listen.
- Encourage all the children to really listen to each other. The first step in language is hearing the spoken word.
- Expand on the child's one-word answer with a complete phrase and then encourage the child to repeat the phrase. "Ball." "Yes, that is a blue ball."
- Encourage verbalization among the children. This means a noisy classroom where children are talking.
- Children may enjoy a buddy system with another child that is bilingual or English speaking.

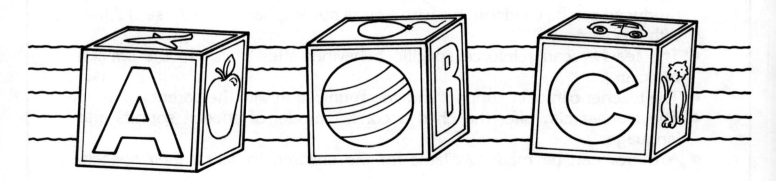

Hearing Impairment

Children with a hearing impairment have the difficult task of learning without the most vital of tools, hearing. Language is acquired naturally and children with a severe deficit must work hard for every gain made.

What to Look for Includes:

- children who speak too loudly or softly
- severe abnormalities of articulation
- very poor attention
- children who say, "What?" "Huh?"
- children who cock their heads to one side
- a sudden jump in attention when presented with a high or low-pitched sound
- children who are very quiet or have shyness when speaking

Teacher Can:

- make visual clues available whenever an oral instruction is given
- be cautious of misleading facial expressions
- make clear movement with your lips
- make direct eye contact with the child and if possible, speak at the child's eye level
- stay stationary when giving instructions and don't turn away from the class and continue the verbal instruction
- try to integrate the visual with the auditory whenever possible
- assure that her face is well lit and without a glare from the light
- assure that the child is correctly positioned if he/she has one ear that operates better than the other
- speak slowly and clearly and use good vocal inflection

Listening is hard work for the able child and may bring on frustration and fatigue for the hearing impaired child. Be sensitive to the demands the classroom situation may put on a hearing impaired child. Allow rest time and time where the stimulation is only visual and not auditory.

135

GA1093

Visually Impaired Children

Children with a visual impairment are in a difficult situation in a world that expects us to see. How many times a day does a teacher say the words *look* and *see*? "Look for the one that is different? Do you see the arrow on the page?" These children must learn to survive, grow and learn in a visual world. Teachers can help to make the transition.

What to Look for Includes:

- children who rub their eyes
- children who have eyes that appear to be crossed
- eyes of children that show random movement
- children who are sensitive to light
- difficulty when the written word is presented
- children who consistently shut one eye or thrust themselves forward to read
- children who complain of headaches or eye pain when doing close work
- children who cannot see at close range or those who have difficulty with distant range

What Can the Teacher Do?

- If the teacher suspects any problems that have not been diagnosed, then the child should be referred for further testing.
- Children with poor vision need to be reinforced with the sense of touch and hearing to enrich the experience.
- If the child has a severe impairment, then always tell the child where you are taking him/her before any movement and verbally support the journey with language cues about the floor and environment that you are walking through.
- Before touching a child with a severe impairment, identify yourself and teach the children to do the same.
- Use experiences and materials to teach that may be familiar to the child and will encourage exploration.
- Encourage freedom of movement whenever possible.
- Use large print or Braille whenever available.

Visually impaired children use sound to give them an orientation to the environment. They may click their tongue or smack their lips to "hear the room." Children with normal vision run to release their energies, and visually impaired children may rock or hop in place. In every situation try to find a way to make the visually impaired child a part of the regular and normal classroom activities. Don't build unnecessary walls for the child but rather be creative at knocking down the walls.

● ● ● ● ● ● ● ● ● ● ●

GA1093